Pract
BULB GROWING

BRIAN LEVERETT

The Crowood Press

First published in 1995 by
The Crowood Press Ltd
Ramsbury, Marlborough
Wiltshire SN8 2HR

British Library Cataloguing-in-Publication Data

A catalogue record for this book is available from the British
Library.

ISBN 1 85223 857 7

Picture Credits
Line-drawings by Claire Upsdale-Jones
Photographs on pages 6, 8, 11, 12, 13, 16 (left), 25 (left and
top right), 32 (left), 34 (left), 37, 38 and 47 (top and bottom
left) are by Brian Leverett; those on pages 2–3, 7, 26, 31
(right), 32 (right), 34 (right), 36, 44 and 48 (left) are by John
Lockwood; those on pages 1, 17, 21, 23, 45, 46, 47 (top right)
and 52 are by Sue Atkinson; those on pages 28 (top), 30, 41,
42, 48 (right) and 56 are by Ian Murray; those on pages 6 (top),
25 (bottom right) and 31 (left) are by M. Robinson; that on
page 28 (bottom) is by Brynphotos; those on pages 16 (right)
and 55 are by David Pike; those on pages 62 and 63 are by
Stephen Taffler.

Typeset in Optima by Chippendale Type Ltd,
Pool-in-Wharfedale, West Yorkshire
Printed and bound by Paramount Printing Group, Hong Kong.
Colour Separation by Next Graphic Limited, Hong Kong.

CONTENTS

1 • WHAT IS A BULB?

Bulbs, Corms and Tubers

The growing of bulbs is the easiest of all forms of gardening: no special skills are required and success is virtually guaranteed. All that you need to do is to put the bulb into the ground and wait for it to flower. Some bulbs do not need soil, they will produce blooms by standing in a glass of water; others, such as colchicums, do not even require water as they will bloom when simply allowed to stand on a shelf. This is all possible because the flower and the leaves are already contained within the bulb itself, ready to burst forth immediately that the correct signals are received. When the leaves emerge they will rapidly turn green as the chlorophyll begins to develop. This acts as a catalyst, converting water and the carbon dioxide of the air into solid materials, which supplement those contained within the bulb itself.

As the leaves begin to emerge the process of forming the next year's bulb commences. Grown naturally in the soil the roots will begin to take up minerals, which the plant needs for a variety of purposes as the new bulb begins to form.

But this is only one type of bulb. The term is used in two ways – in a strict botanical sense to describe the true bulbs, and in a loose generic manner to cover a wide group of plants that pass the dormant season by storing food for next year's growth in a variety of different forms of swollen stem and root tissue. To all but the trained, distinguishing between the various structures can be confusing and is unnecessary – it is the growing of the plants that is important. In this book we will be looking at bulbs in their widest sense and use the term as it is applied in everyday conversation. Yet in order to understand how we may get the best out of every plant and grow and propagate them successfully, it is advantageous to appreciate the differences between the structures commonly referred to as bulbs.

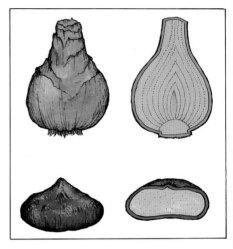

Bulbs and corms are distinct structures. Bulbs are simply underground buds while corms are food stores with external buds.

A *true bulb* is a group of old leaf bases from the previous year around an embryonic bud and new leaves. Basically the bulb is the bud itself with the food store an inherent part of that bud. Included within this group are daffodils and narcissi, tulips, snowdrops and also onions and shallots, and the ornamental members of this family, the alliums.

Pseudobulbs are false bulbs that resemble the real thing but are simply food stores capable of forming shoots. The term is most frequently applied to the growths produced by orchids.

Bulbils are small immature bulbs that develop in the leaf joints of lilies. The term bulbil can also be applied to the small growths around the bases of larger (true) bulbs. In neither case will they flower the season following the year in which they were produced, but they can be grown on to bloom in future years.

Corms are swollen roots with one or more buds attached. These buds, rather than the large structure, contain the

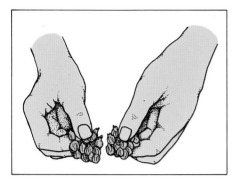

Tiny bulbils which grow around the base of large bulbs can be carefully removed and grown on to produce new plants.

embryonic flowers and leaves. Corms die back after flowering; the part which had contained the stored food contracts to a dense hard pad of dead material and a new corm develops above it. Crocuses and gladioli are two of the best known corms.

Tubers are thickened stems, consisting of a large food supply with a limited number of buds coming from it. Tubers can take on various forms: cyclamen and begonia

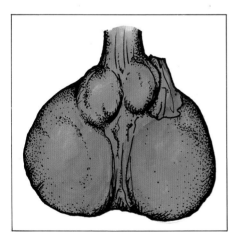

New corms form above the old ones; its work having been done, it gradually withers away.

tubers are flat and increase in size each year, the buds emerging from the top of the flat, dish-shaped structure; dahlias, on the other hand, develop several finger-like growths which increase in size and number each year with the buds being situated at the point where the fingers join last season's stem. The tubers are usually only capable of producing directly a limited number of buds, but these growth buds, once clear of the roots, may continue to produce an apparently inexhaustible supply of flower buds, as in the case of dahlias. There are exceptions. A cyclamen tuber seems capable of forming a limitless number of flower and leaf buds during its season.

What all of these structures that we loosely call bulbs have in common is that they make up the whole plant during the dormant season when the perennial must naturally rest.

Moreover, they are a vegetative means of propagation, which means that plants produced by division of bulbs (or any of the other structures described) by the means explained in this book will produce clones identical in every way to the single parent. Seeds, which are the result of sexual reproduction requiring two parents, may lead to totally unpredictable results. The bulb-like structures are the only means of reproducing named varieties that have well-defined features. Bulbs can be grown in any location, providing that it is reasonably well drained, on acid or chalk soils, in open or shaded aspect. Flowers in the first season are virtually guaranteed by the food supply built up in the previous year, but they need care and attention if they are to develop viable bulbs for future years, and this can have a profound effect on your choice of site and method of culture.

Research has shown that the true bulbs, particularly narcissi and tulips, must be left to grow uninterrupted for at least six weeks after they have flowered. Remember it is during this time that next season's new

The short iris pumila, which grows from 15-30cm (6-12in) is ideal for planting in rockeries. It is available in a range of the most delicate colours.

embyronic plant is building up and it is the most critical stage in the growth cycle. If the process is prematurely stopped or the food supply is cut off, the developing plant will not be fully formed and will almost certainly go 'blind', not producing any flowers in future years. Often we site bulbs in primary locations where they will be seen to full advantage, but such areas are required for replanting with summer bedding almost immediately that the spring flowers have died. With the need to sustain constant interest in the garden there is pressure to replant the site as soon as the spring flowers have died. To be able to do this and ensure that the bulbs bloom next year they must be transplanted to a nursery bed.

Even with mixed beds and other sites not needed immediately for replanting, the

The formal spring flowerbed rivals the most dazzling displays of the summertime.

leaves of flowers such as daffodils can be extremely untidy, but unless you are transplanting them they must be left undisturbed.

Do not cut back the leaves, or bend them over and tie them back. Either method will reduce the leaves' ability to return all of the food that they have generated to the new bulb that is developing below. Where the leaves have been damaged new bulbs will form but they will be too small to produce any flowers in the ensuing year.

After the flowers on bulbous plants have died, always pick out the ovaries, the small spherical swellings behind the base of the flower, to stop the developing seeds from draining the plant's energy. The only exceptions to this are naturalized flowers such as snowdrops and bluebells, where the seeds which will scatter naturally, germinate and help the spread of the bulbs. Do not allow the ovaries of naturalized members of the daffodil family to remain on the stems, as the seedlings, which can take many years to reach flowering size, will almost certainly have reverted to the smaller, less spectacular wild species.

Naturalized bulbs – those that are allowed to grow undisturbed, spreading as they may – are an important landscaping feature in the less formal spring garden. Planted where they can grow without interference the bulbs rapidly spread to create a natural-looking feature, blending in with the surroundings. But naturalizing requires careful choice of site. Most spring bulbs will have completed the critical part of their growing cycle before the deciduous trees have regained their leaves. We can make use of this by planting bulbs around the base of ornamental and fruit trees, thereby utilizing areas that would otherwise be unproductive and providing colour in a locality denuded of greenery.

Bulbs naturalized in grass have a certain empathy with the landscape but you must not plant them in tiptop lawns. The need to

The crocus is an ideal bulb for planting in lawns where it flowers before the grass has had the opportunity to grow tall. Early flowering forms will have died back in time to allow the grass to be cut during the spring.

allow the leaves to die back naturally will stop you from cutting any part of the lawn that still has bulbs growing in it, even though they finished flowering several weeks before. Where lawns are left uncut the coarser grasses naturally take over, so naturalizing is restricted to rough-grassed areas.

Tubers continue to develop throughout the growing season and immediately that this has come to its natural conclusion, or that the top growth has been cut down by the frost (as occurs with dahlias), the swollen stems should be brought inside and dried off prior to storing.

Classification

Daffodils, tulips, dahlias and many other varieties are usually classified according to certain characteristics that the flowers possess, or according to the wild species from which they were derived. In this book the classification is that generally used but descriptions have been modified where appropriate to avoid unnecessary confusion. Only those classifications that include bulbs readily available to and widely grown by the general public are included.

You will need to go to a specialist supplier to obtain bulbs of lachenalia, which is surprising as they make excellent pot plants and deserve to be far more popular.

Purchasing Bulbs

A very wide range of bulbs is available for sale from garden centres, which will usually also seek out and obtain any special varieties that you may require. Many have experts on hand only too happy to provide you with any advice you might need. A large number of non-specialist retailing agents also sell bulbs. To cater for the increased interest in gardening they are offering an ever wider range, but the majority are unlikely to be able to provide for any unusual requirements or to have expert staff available to help you with your gardening problems. It is always best to buy the bulbs as soon as they are available as that way you get the best choice.

Bulbs are often sold prepacked in small transparent plastic bags. Remove them from the bag and store them in a cool, dry place if you do not intend to plant immediately. Allowed to remain in the bag, in the warm, relatively dark, growth-friendly conditions, the bulb will begin to shoot, producing weak, yellow, spindly tissue that is unlikely to recover and produce strong healthy growth. At the same time the emerging shoot will drain moisture and nutrients from the bulb. When purchasing packeted bulbs always ensure that long growths have not started to develop, although depending on time and species, short, firm, well-advanced buds may be normal. Also check that the buds have not become detached from a corm or tuber as a result of rough handling, as it may not have the capacity to generate fresh buds.

When purchasing loose bulbs always examine them carefully to ensure that there are no signs of damage. Check the surface to make sure that there are no black pitting marks, which could be the start of fungal infection, and gently feel the bulb. A bulb in prime condition will be firm to the touch without any signs of damage or abrasion.

The largest range of bulbs is obtainable by mail order. Suppliers' addresses can be found in advertisements placed in gardening magazines or in newspapers during the planting season.

2 • PROPAGATION

The propagation of bulbs is an easy, cheap way of increasing your stock. As well as their role as storage organs, bulbs are also nature's back-up means of reproduction. Their role is to increase the size of the individual clumps, whereas that of the far lighter and smaller seeds is to be transported away to form new colonies of plants. Seeds may take several years to produce flowering plants; bulbs and root divisions often flower the following season.

Bulbs, which bring about vegetative reproduction, are clones having only one parent; the offspring are identical in every way to the mother plant. Seeds are the result of sexual reproduction with two parents each contributing their own genes. It is the fertilization by pollen of one plant of the ovaries of another that brings about the mix of genes that can result in the formation of new varieties. Species – wild or natural forms of plants – tend to have identical major genes and any seeds gathered from these will produce offspring apparently identical with their wild ancestors. Varieties artificially bred by man will have dissimilar genes and it is from these that the new varieties result. But do not rush out collecting seeds from garden varieties of bulbs, since random crosses almost invariably

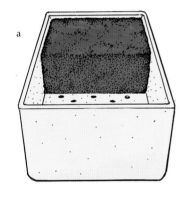

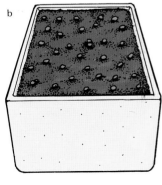

Growing bulbous plants from seed. (a) Make holes in the bottom of a margarine tub or similar container, and fill with an open peat-based compost. Thoroughly moisten the mixture and allow to drain. (b) Sprinkle the seeds thinly over the surface of the compost. Cover with compost according to the instructions on the seed packet. (c) Cover the container with a clear polythene bag. Stand in a temperature of 15°C (60°F), or the temperature specified on the seed packet.

(a) Recently germinated seedlings will be crowded together. Place a spatula under them and gently lift them. (b) Separate the individual seedlings, handling them by their leaves to avoid damaging the delicate stems. (c) Replant the seedlings well spaced out in a seed box. (d) When the seedlings are about 10cm (4in) tall, transplant singly into a flower pot filled with compost.

result in the plants reverting back to common, less spectacular forms. Most worthwhile new plants are the result of very careful scientific breeding plans. The practical rule with seeds is to gather and grow only seeds of true wild species such as bluebells, snowdrops or wild daffodils (Lent lilies) for naturalizing. Do not gather seed from the wild (this is an offence), you may purchase specially raised seeds from controlled crosses such as freesias or gloxinias; these give predictable results as both parents are known, as is the appearance of the seedlings. But do not save the seeds of these special crosses, as their offspring may be unpredictable and unspectacular. You can of course propagate the bulbs, which will be identical to the parent.

Propagation of Spring-Flowering Species

Daffodils

Lift bulbs not intended for naturalizing and separate the offsets growing by the side of the main bulbs. These will not flower in the following year, but can be grown on in nursery beds. Providing that the soil is rich and they are fed throughout the spring they will flower during the following year. After that time they may be transplanted to their permanent positions. Naturalized clumps should be lifted every five years. As well as

Modern hybrid daffodils can be obtained in many and varied forms.

increasing the number of groups use the opportunity to divide the individual groups in order to reduce the congestion and competition for nutrients in the soil.

Crocuses

To propagate, lift the corms immediately that the leaves have died back and remove the small cormlets that develop around the sides. Plant in any suitable location where undisturbed they will flower in two to three years. Where additional stock is not required the corms may be left undisturbed virtually indefinitely, and the flowering clump will become progressively larger each season.

Tulips

Lift the bulbs after the leaves have died back completely. You will find small bulblets in addition to the main bulb. Remove and grow these on in a nursery bed. Harvest again after the leaves have died back in the following spring. Replant in the autumn in the chosen flowering area.

Snowdrops

Allow bulbs to remain undisturbed for about four years, then immediately that they have ceased flowering lift, divide and replant the groups, using the 'in the green' technique. Seed heads will hang down and can be gathered. Save the seed and sow in a pot in the greenhouse in mid-autumn. Allow the seedlings to die down in the summer and give water the following autumn. Allow the seedlings to remain in the pot until they have flowered, then transplant outdoors.

Leucojum or Snowflake

Leave bulbs in the ground to divide and self propagate. Raise the bulbs from time to time to divide (about every four to five years) and replant.

Hyacinths

These seem to be very reluctant to form new bulbs, in the wild tending to depend mainly upon seed to increase the numbers. However, hyacinths can be induced to create bulbils at sites of artificial damage to the base plate. Simply cut a cross in the plate before planting. Dig up the bulb immediately that the leaves have died back and you will see that a number of bulbils will have formed around the base plate. Remove them and grow on in a nursery bed until they are of flowering size.

Hyacinths
Planting time   Early to mid-autumn.
Aspect   Full sun or very light shade.
Space   20-25cm (9in).
Planting depth   15cm (6in).
Height   20-25cm (9in).
Flowering period   Mid- to late spring.
Uses   As an edge to a border or grouped together to form a permanent feature in a mixed bed.
Propagation   Mainly by seed.
Pests and diseases   Can be attacked by narcissus fly (*see* 'Daffodils') and may be infected with a virus which causes the leaves to be marked with yellow spots and streaks.

Alliums

Unlike most other bulbs, which are divided after they have flowered, large clumps of alliums should be dug up and divided as soon as the bulbs come into growth during the spring.

Being species they will grow true from seed. The seed, which is spherical, black and hard and resembles small lead shot, should be gathered as soon as it is ripe. Sow in seed pans in a cold greenhouse in mid-autumn. After a year, the grass-like seedlings will have become quite large, and can be planted out of doors in a nursery bed. They will produce flowering-size bulbs in another one or two years.

Fritillaries

Propagation tends to be rather slow. Fritillaries will produce small offsets, which, given time, will develop into flowering-size bulbs. In general the bulbs should not be disturbed but they can be lifted, the bulbils removed and then grown in pots until they reach flowering size.

Anemones

To maintain top-quality flowers the tubers should be lifted every other year, the offshoots removed and the large tuberous roots divided with a sharp knife before replanting.

Muscari

Self-sown seeds will naturally propagate the species, which rapidly increases the size of the clumps. Seeds may be gathered when ripe and sown in a pan in the cold greenhouse for transplanting into a nursery bed the following year. Clumps may be divided by waiting until the leaves have turned yellow in mid-summer. Lift, divide and replant.

Bluebells growing together with the less common pink and white bells.

Bluebells

Propagate by gathering the hard, round, black seeds and sowing them, in mid-summer, as soon as they are ripe. Or you can divide and transplant the clumps 'in the green' immediately that they have flowered.

Propagation of Summer-Flowering Species

There are more diverse forms of summer-flowering bulbs, employing a wide range of different propagation techniques.

Dahlias

Propagation of dahlias is important not only for increasing the stock but for stimulating the plant into the production of fresh youthful growth. There are two methods of increasing the stock – either inducing the tubers to shoot, removing the shoots and encouraging them into growth, or division of the tuber itself, which will then form new plants through the bud eyes at the neck of the root. For the first method, however, you will need access to a greenhouse.

SHOOT PROPAGATION

Place the tubers upright in a seed-tray in a greenhouse in early spring and spray daily with tepid water to encourage them to shoot. Allow the shoots to grow until they are about 10cm (4in) long then cut them off as near to the point where they emerge from the tuber as possible. Trim the cutting with a knife just below the lowest leaf joint. Remove the bottom pair of leaves and dip the cutting into a combined hormone powder and fungicide before planting individually into 7.5cm (3in) pots. Cover the pot and shoot with a polythene bag and keep in the greenhouse. From mid-spring onwards the cuttings can be hardened off, before planting out when all danger of frost has passed.

Use simple root division to propagate, if you do not possess a greenhouse.

ROOT DIVISION

Stand the roots upright in a seed-tray in a frost-free room but do not spray with water. By the middle of April the shoots will be clearly seen emerging from the buds situated around the area where the individual tubers joined last year's stem. With a sharp knife cut down through the old dead stem, leaving at least three buds on each piece and retaining with them part of the fibrous tissue together with some complete 'fingers' of the fleshy swollen root. It is very important that the latter do not become detached, as they are only food reserves incapable of generating buds and will simply die without the piece at the base of the stem. Any open cuts should be dusted with flowers of sulphur and the plants allowed to continue to develop shoots before being hardened off and planted outside.

Gladioli

Gladioli form one or two new large corms in place of the one involved in the current year's growth, which will remain as a hard

The small cormlets that appear at the base of the gladiolus corm can be removed and grown on to form full-sized corms.

fibrous pad at the base of the new corms. In addition, cormlets about 4-5mm in diameter are seen around the main corm when it is lifted in the autumn. Employing a similar technique to that used for the flowering-size corms, grow the cormlets in the following spring and harvest in the autumn. The corms will be large enough to flower the next season or the one after.

Lilies

The bulbs of many varieties of lily consist of several scales grouped round the centre. Removed and potted on separately each scale will grow on to make a bulb.

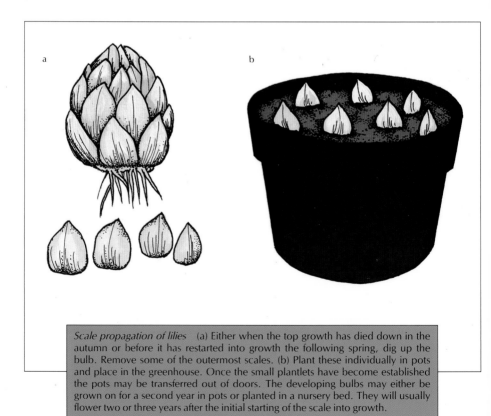

Scale propagation of lilies (a) Either when the top growth has died down in the autumn or before it has restarted into growth the following spring, dig up the bulb. Remove some of the outermost scales. (b) Plant these individually in pots and place in the greenhouse. Once the small plantlets have become established the pots may be transferred out of doors. The developing bulbs may either be grown on for a second year in pots or planted in a nursery bed. They will usually flower two or three years after the initial starting of the scale into growth.

The hybrids of some species of lily produce bulbils, small round vegetative growths in the leaf axils. Delay gathering until the leaves have turned yellow. Immediately place the bulbils in a seed-tray in the greenhouse. When the shoots are 5cm (2in) long, transfer them to individual flowerpots and grow on as described for leaf scale propagation.

Irises

The rhizomous irises or flag lilies are increased by the division of the thick, horizontal, ground-hugging stem.

Propagate immediately that the flowering period is over. With a sharp knife make a cut 7-10cm (3-4in) from the end of the rhizome. Lift the detached piece of rhizome complete with the root attached. Reduce the top growth by half to restrict the loss of water before planting in a new position.

Increase the bulbous rooted irises by lifting and dividing the bulbs after the plants have flowered.

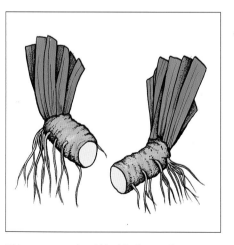

Rhizomous iris should be lifted every three to four years, the rhizome divided into pieces 10cm (4in) in length and replanted. Reduce the height of the leaves by half to minimize the water loss.

Nerines

These are propagated by lifting and dividing the bulbs.

Colchicums

Propagate by removing the secondary corms that form around the main corm.

Propagation of Tender Bulbs

Tender bulbs are grown in very strictly controlled conditions, particularly of temperature and moisture, and in many cases it is more practical to grow them initially from seed. In future years the bulbs can either be grown on or new vigorous specimens raised from seed. Usually grown as single pot plants the method of culture is particularly suited to growing F_1 hybrids from seeds. These are of better form and colour than the species normally obtained by this method.

Amaryllis (Hippeastrum)

These can be propagated from home-gathered seed, although the hybrid varieties will not breed true. Allow the seed head to develop and ripen. Immediately that the pods have acquired the colour of brown paper, gather and sow the large, flat seeds. Until the seedlings have actually produced a flower, which may take four to five years depending upon the conditions in which they are grown, they do not require a rest period. They should be maintained in growth all the year round by watering and giving a weekly feed with a liquid fertilizer at half the recommended strength. The flowers may be white, pale pink through to deepest carmine, or bicoloured, usually white shot with pinks or red.

Vegetatively they may be propagated by removing and potting separately the

Amaryllis
Planting time   Early autumn to mid-winter.
Position   Heated greenhouse, conservatory or lounge.
Planting depth   Deep enough so that the neck of the bulb is just protruding.
Height   60cm (2ft).
Flowering period   Mid-winter to mid-spring.
Propagation   As the bulbs grow they will develop secondary bulbs on the sides. When these reach flowering size, they may be removed and potted on separately.
Repotting   Not necessary every year. Aim to repot, change the soil and divide as necessary, which is usually every four to five years.

secondary bulbs that develop on the sides of the main bulb.

Freesias

Any bulblets may be removed before repotting during late summer. Named varieties must be propagated from corms, but a range of colours can be obtained from seeds, which unlike many bulbous plants will yield flowers after just six months.

RAISING FREESIAS FROM SEED

Soak the seeds in tepid water overnight. Sow thinly in late spring or early summer in a seed pan. Place in a position in the greenhouse where they will receive maximum daylight. When the grass-like seedlings are 5cm (2in) long, transplant four to six into a 12.7cm (5in) pot. Stake and

maintain in a well-ventilated position in the greenhouse. From mid-autumn onwards maintain the temperature at 5°C.

Gloxinias

Good quality blooms can be obtained from seed sown in a peat-based compost in late winter and maintained at a temperature of 18°C (65°F) until germination is complete and thereafter at 15°C (60°F). The seedlings sown in pans should be pricked out individually into 15cm (6in) pots as soon as they are large enough to handle. This technique will give you dramatic yet unpredictable colours.

Vegetative propagation is by division of the tuber. Stand the tubers in a warm room until early spring. When the buds have developed sufficiently to be clearly seen, cut the tuber with a sharp knife in such a way that each piece has at least two growing shoots. Dust the exposed surface with flowers of sulphur to prevent infection by fungal diseases (*see* method given below for the division of begonia tubers).

Gloxinias
Planting time   Late winter.
Planting depth   Upper surface of the bulb should be exposed.
Height   15–20cm (6–8in).
Flowering period   Mid-summer to early autumn.
Propagation   By seed.
Repotting   Each year.

Begonias

Begonia tubers usually develop up to six shoots, but you only require two to produce strong healthy plants. The extra shoots may be removed and grown, planted and allowed to develop roots, or the tuber itself can be divided.

SHOOT PROPAGATION

This allows you to produce very large plants as all the tuber's energies can be directed into one or two stems after the additional shoots have been removed to create rooted cuttings. Allow the shoots to grow to 7-10cm (3-4in), then with a sharp knife sever the shoot at the point where it joins the tuber. Dip the shoots in a combined hormone rooting powder and fungicide and insert around the edge of a flowerpot filled with soaked and drained compost. Cover the cuttings and pot with a clear polythene bag and place in a warm position on the greenhouse shelf. Maintain the humid conditions that encourage rooting by keeping the cuttings in the plastic bag until they have rooted, then transplant to individual 15cm (6in) flowerpots.

TUBER DIVISION

This is the standard procedure for division of tubers of this type. Where tubers have become very large and you require no more than medium-size plants for bedding purposes or pendulous varieties for hanging baskets, the corms may be divided when the shoots are 1cm (½in) long.

Cut the tuber into two parts with a sharp knife so that each of the halves now contains at least two shoots. Dust the cut surface with flowers of sulphur to stop fungal infections. Plant each piece individually in a 12cm (5in) flowerpot. Keep the compost damp at all stages and give a weekly feed from the time that the first buds form.

The begonias are then grown on either in the greenhouse or outside in beds.

Cyclamen hederifolium, a hardy species which grows well in any rock garden.

Cyclamen

Cyclamen tubers, unlike gloxinias and begonias, cannot be divided easily, neither do they produce offsets or bulbils. Propagation must be by seed. Seeds may be sown in late winter to produce plants that will flower the following autumn. For winter sowings it will be necessary to maintain a temperature of 15°C (60°F) during the germination and seedling stage. Alternatively you may sow them in the greenhouse during early autumn, when they will germinate at the ambient temperature, but the seedlings will require a temperature of 15°C (60°F) throughout the winter. Such plants will produce larger corms for flowering a year after sowing.

Pleiones

The small offsets that form around the base of the pseudobulb should be removed when the plants are being repotted. Small pseudobulbs will also form on the plants themselves above ground level. These should be detached and grown on separately in a pot until they reach flowering size.

3 • CULTIVATION

Most spring bulbs are on sale from late summer to late autumn. During this period the plant is dormant, but it is unnatural for them to remain out of the ground for prolonged periods. Ideally you should plant the bulbs as soon as you receive them, but to avoid disturbing summer bedding plants and keep them in position as long as possible you will probably find it more practical to set them out in mid-autumn. Do not delay beyond this date. Although you are unlikely to see much activity above ground level until mid-winter, in the soil the bulbs will be receiving the triggers that start them growing. By the end of autumn they will have a well-established root system. Late planting means poorer roots with a reduced capacity to take up nutrients, and so weaker bulbs for next year.

Bulbs have a very special role to play in winter gardens made up of heathers and conifers, with their cones and shoots providing interest and colour at a time when the landscape is drab. Here single bulbs or groups of three of snowdrops, crocuses or miniature daffodils (such as 'Hooped Petticoat') will create a focal point in a similar way to a jewel worn against a costume, providing eye-catching brightness without taking over from the main feature. An even wider range of bulbs, including the miniature irises, performs a similar function in the alpine garden.

Special planters make planting bulbs much easier, producing the ideal, non-pointed, flat-bottomed hole for the bulb to rest in.

The very thin-skinned bulbs – such as snowdrops, bluebells and the tuberous winter aconite – soon dry out if they are kept out of the ground for prolonged periods, and the best results are not obtained from autumn plantings. These should all be transplanted 'in the green', a process consisting of transplanting the bulbs during flowering or just after.

Grouping Bulbs

Before setting out the bulbs decide exactly how you wish to position them. Bulbs do not lend themselves to regimentation in the way that bedding plants do. The two main exceptions to this are hyacinths when grown as an edging to a border and tulips intermingled with wallflowers. If you want them to look natural, even in a bed they should be grouped together. For small groups use an odd number of bulbs with one bulb nearest the observer, a second

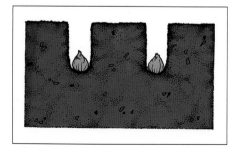

Bulbs should be correctly positioned by having the base set on firm soil with no air gaps beneath them which could trap water.

row containing two bulbs behind that and four bulbs behind the second row. With smaller bulbs and corms such as crocuses, allow them to drop gently on to the ground from a height of 60cm (2ft) and plant them where they fall. This tends to give a pleasing natural distribution. Very tall bulbs such as crown imperials and the larger alliums should be grown as solitary subjects at the back of the beds.

Feeding

Although the bulbs will make the majority of the food that they require by photosynthesis, they also require minerals, which they take in through their roots. Potash helps form hard, strong growth and a light scattering of sulphate of potash is beneficial if placed around the site of established spring bulbs during autumn, when they are forming their roots. Delay feeding a general purpose fertilizer until the following spring. The extra nitrogen that these contain can cause rapid growth, which is no problem as the weather begins to warm up and the hours of daylight increase, but if the feed were to be given in the colder, darker autumn, it could stimulate the bulbs into producing soft premature shoots, incapable of withstanding the severe weather ahead.

Growing Bulbs in Containers

Bulbs are particularly suitable for growing in containers or hanging baskets, which are the out-of-doors equivalent of growing bulbs in bowls. To achieve the best displays include other bright subjects such as polyanthuses and pansies, which are in flower at the same time. Baskets and containers for spring displays should be prepared in mid-autumn.

Containers varying greatly in size, height and shape allow far greater latitude than do the standardized baskets. Any receptacle of

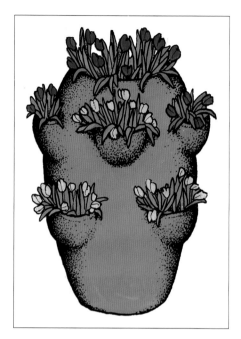

A wide range of containers may be used for planting bulbs.

suitable appearance, that is physically capable of retaining the compost and is provided with drainage holes can be used for growing bulbs. Let your imagination run riot, there is no limit to what can be adapted to the purpose. Terracotta pots and half beer barrels are amongst the most suitable of the many containers available from garden centres.

First check that there are drainage holes – you may need to create these yourself before some of the containers can be used. These are necessary so that the winter rains can escape from the compost, otherwise the bulbs are liable to rot. Furthermore, if water is trapped in the soil, it can form a solid ice block during severe frosts. Cover the holes with inverted pieces of broken ceramic material in order that the compost is retained as the water runs away.

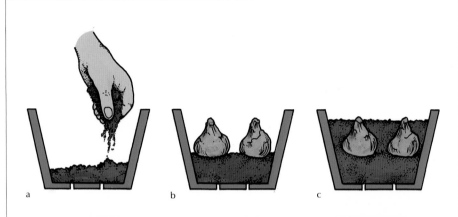

a   b   c

Planting bulbs for forcing The simplest way to plant bulbs in bowls is in a single layer. Containers with drainage holes are always preferable to those without, but there are several very pleasant vessels, which are decorative in themselves, which do not have holes in the base. These can be used, but you must remember not to overwater as where moisture cannot escape this can lead to the development of conditions which will cause the bulbs to rot. Do not mix different varieties of bulb in the same bowl. They often flower at slightly different times, which does not extend the life of the bowl but creates an unharmonious mixture of buds, flowers in full bloom and dead and dying blooms. Far better to extend the range by preparing several different bowls, each containing one distinct variety of bulb. (a) Place a layer of compost at the base of the container. (b) Plant the bulbs close together – they may be touching each other – as they do not need extra space in the way that seedlings do. (c) Fill with soil so that their necks are just protruding.

Where the containers are particularly deep, extra drainage can be provided by means of a layer of gravel at the base. Stand the container on blocks or bricks to help the water to run away. Fill the container to within 5cm (2in) of the top with compost. Plant (depending upon size) with a single type of bulb or a mixture, together with annual or perennial plants. When planning a larger container remember to include a mixture of bulbs that will bloom over a prolonged season to complement the other plants that bloom for several weeks. Alternatively, you may prepare several containers, site them in the display area when in bud and remove when the blooms are dead.

Making a Hanging Basket

To make up a hanging basket for the growing of spring bulbs, first line an open mesh-type container with sphagnum moss, before filling it to near the brim with a peat or coir-based compost. For the bulbous subjects choose short types, as tall plants such as standard daffodils look out of place in a basket. Generally, use no more than one type of bulb per basket. These will need to be planted near to the centre of the container to provide sufficient depth for the bulbs to achieve the necessary anchorage. Evenly space four of the larger subjects like hyacinths or six smaller plants such as the

Elegant containers show bulbs off to their best advantage. Here the white blooms complement the stone-coloured container.

kaufmanniana tulips in the compost and intermingle the smaller fibrous-rooted plants between the bulbs. Once planted, the hanging basket may be kept in the cold greenhouse and placed out of doors when it is ready to bloom. Alternatively the basket may be sited in its permanent position at the time that it is prepared.

Growing Spring Bulbs for Cutting

Simply as a bunch or as an indispensable item of a floral decoration, spring bulb flowers are ideal for brightening up the home. Small numbers of flowers may be selectively gathered, larger amounts are easily grown as a crop. Select a well-drained site with an open sunny aspect: part of the vegetable plot is ideal. During September, plant daffodil or narcissi bulbs in rows, in soil which was manured for the previous summer's crop. Space the bulbs 7-10cm (3-4in) apart in rows 45cm (1½ft) apart. If space is not available or simply to brighten up the area in the springtime the bulbs can also be grown in clumps at various locations around the plot. Allow the bulbs to grow naturally. Picking the blooms will not damage the bulbs, but do not cut the leaves, which will stop the bulbs from producing flowers the following year. Allow the plants to finish growing. As soon as the leaves have died back, dig up the bulbs, remove the soil and dry by allowing them to stand on a piece of hessian in the sun during the daytime, bringing them inside if there is any danger of rain. When the bulbs are thoroughly dry, they should be stored in a cool, dry place. Make sure that the bulbs cannot be found and eaten by mice, which are particularly partial to them. The dried, lifted bulbs may be propagated by separating in the autumn and either grown on in the vegetable plot as a crop again or some can be transferred to the flower beds. Bulbs raised in this way will be of similar quality to those purchased.

TRANSPLANTING BULBS AFTER FLOWERING

Select an open, well-drained site that is visually unobtrusive. Dig a trench to the same depth at which the bulbs were growing, and line with nylon mesh. This is important to ensure that you are able to find the bulbs for replanting in the following autumn when all the greenery has died back. Plant the bulbs in the trench and backfill in around them with soil. Allow the bulbs to finish growing. Once the leaves have turned yellow, died and will come away in the hand with a gentle pull, carefully dig out behind the nylon mesh, gather up the material and separate the bulbs from the soil.

4 • FAVOURITE SPRING BULBS

There are many bulbous plants which are planted in the autumn to bloom in the spring. Every year the number which are readily available increases, while the old favourites retain their popularity.

Daffodils and Narcissi

Daffodils and narcissi are members of the same group; they are all referred to as daffodils by the showman or all as narcissi by the botanist. More commonly the term daffodils is used loosely to describe those varieties whose trumpet is as long or longer than the petals. Those with shorter trumpets are described as narcissi. Each year both forms become increasingly popular, and

are so widespread that they dominate the spring landscape more than any other flower. Each year sees a far greater range on sale at the cheaper end of the market. You can afford to be adventurous in your choice and need no longer be restricted to the three or four forms and very limited colour range which were once all that was available.

All daffodils are derived from the wild *Narcissus* species, which has a range of many different flower shapes and sizes. Hybridizing has made a choice of colours available, which for the petals may be yellow through to white, with the cup, corona or trumpet being yellow to white or from orange red through to pink. In some varieties the stems carry only one bloom, whereas in others they are multiflowered.

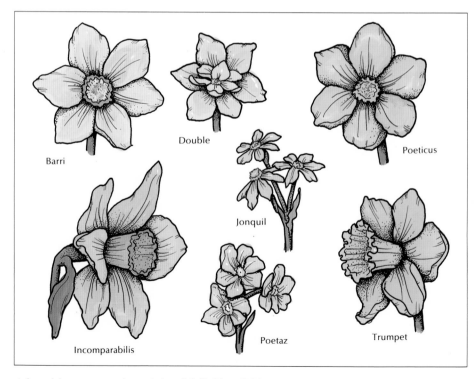

Barri

Double

Poeticus

Jonquil

Incomparabilis

Poetaz

Trumpet

A few of the many popular varieties of daffodil available.

Indoors or out, narcissi are ideal for growing in bowls.

As with many plants the flowers may be single or double and miniature forms are also known. True wild species of narcissus are not grown except for naturalizing. Many thousands of named varieties of garden origin have been registered, but only a fraction of these are on sale to the general gardener. Nevertheless the range is so diverse that consideration should be given to growing some of the less familiar types. The daffodil cultivars are classified in twelve different divisions, but this only affects exhibitors. The groups most suited to growing in the garden are listed below.

Popular Varieties

Most popular are the daffodils in which the central cup or corona is longer than the petals. They have only one flower per stem.

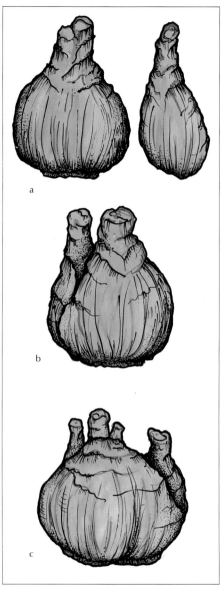

Daffodil bulbs are described according to their noses or necks from which the shoots develop. (a) A single-nosed bulb. (b) A double-nosed bulb. (c) A mother-nosed bulb consisting of more than two noses.

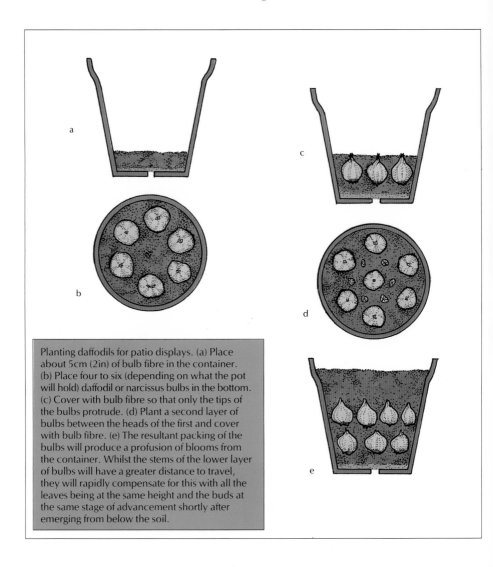

Planting daffodils for patio displays. (a) Place about 5cm (2in) of bulb fibre in the container. (b) Place four to six (depending on what the pot will hold) daffodil or narcissus bulbs in the bottom. (c) Cover with bulb fibre so that only the tips of the bulbs protrude. (d) Plant a second layer of bulbs between the heads of the first and cover with bulb fibre. (e) The resultant packing of the bulbs will produce a profusion of blooms from the container. Whilst the stems of the lower layer of bulbs will have a greater distance to travel, they will rapidly compensate for this with all the leaves being at the same height and the buds at the same stage of advancement shortly after emerging from below the soil.

The colours range from the self yellows and self whites to whites with yellow centres and yellow or white outer petals with pink centres.

The large cupped narcissi are of the same general shape as the daffodils, with a central cup that is over a third of the length of the petals and has only one flower per stem.

The third group is made up of the small cupped daffodils in which the corona is less than a third of the length of the petals. They have only one flower per stem.

The fourth group consists of the doubles, which have variously shaped coronas and usually incomplete double trumpets. There may be one or many flowers to a stem.

The *triandrus* daffodils are less widely grown; the representative of this group most frequently found in cultivation is 'Thalia', a white with a trumpet just over two thirds of the length of the petals. The petals are much thinner than those of the daffodils and are very slightly swept back, creating an open bloom. This type carries only one bloom per stem.

Cyclamineus narcissi are more difficult to obtain, but are well worth seeking out. They have long, forward-drooping trumpets, which are swept back in similar style to the cyclamen from which they take their name.

The jonquils are characterized by their rounded stems, which carry one to three flowers.

The *tazetta* are the earliest flowering of all daffodils and are multiheaded. The extra-

'Thalia', a cyclamineus narcissus with swept-back petals.

early 'Paper White' is widely grown both for cut flowers and indoors in bowls.

The *poeticus* or poet's daffodil is characterized by the pure white of the petals and the flat central cup, which is reduced virtually

Daffodils
Planting time   Late summer to mid-autumn.
Aspect   Sun or partial shade.
Space   10-20cm (4-8in) apart depending upon variety.
Planting depth   7.5-10cm (3-4in).
Triandrus and cyclamineus varieties 5cm (2in).
Miniatures 4-5cm (1½-2in).
Height   Most standard varieties 30cm (1ft).
Miniatures 15cm (6in).
Flowering period   Early to mid-spring.
Uses   Bedding, naturalizing, cut flowers and growing in bowls.
Propagation   By offsets.
Pests and diseases   Narcissus fly, and the fungal infection narcissus fire.

The low-growing Narcissus romieuxii is one of the most delicate of the early spring flowers which can add interest either to an alpine garden or to a collection of heathers and dwarf conifers.

to a disc. Two popular forms are 'Actaea' and 'Pheasant's Eye'.

There is also a miscellaneous group, which includes all the miniature varieties, which have a diverse range of shapes. Some are broadly similar to the more familiar larger forms and others, such as the 'Yellow-Hooped Petticoat', have no comparable version amongst the standards.

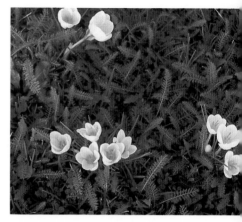

Crocuses exist in several different forms; a variety of colours and shapes can be in flower from mid-winter to late spring. By careful selection of suitable species it is possible to have crocuses in bloom for a third of the year.

Daffodil bulbs not intended for naturalizing should be lifted in mid-summer, cleaned and divided.

For naturalizing in large areas use either the native wild daffodil or Lent lily *(N. pseudonarcissus)* or the swept back *N. cyclamineus.* For smaller areas choose any of the cultivated varieties of the all-yellow or all-white trumpet daffodils or a variety such as 'Actaea', which is one of the few varieties containing a red pigment capable of developing a natural appearance. When naturalizing, always plant about ten bulbs together; grouped in this way they will afford extra protection to each other against the wind, which in exposed areas may break the stems of solitary specimens.

Crocuses

Crocus flowers consist of a tube starting below the ground and opening to six oval petals. There are several different species originating from Europe and Asia, where they are naturally found on high ground. Ideally suited to alpine gardens, they are also generally successful on any well-drained soil. In recent years several different kinds of crocus have become widely available, and whilst there is no general classification in the way that there is for those flowers developed for exhibition purposes, the variations of shape, height, flowering size and time will depend upon the species. The true species, the form which exists in the wild, or naturally occurring sports are widely grown, as are some garden-raised cultivars, especially of the larger forms. The most popular kinds of crocus are listed below.

Popular Varieties

Crocus chrysanthus – the 7-8cm (3in) bowl-shaped flowers are produced in late winter. The wild form is yellow and many other yellow and purple hybrids have been developed. The leaves are of a similar height to the flowers.

C. laevigatus – one of the earliest of all winter/spring bulbs. At only 5cm (2in) tall it is ideal for placing under small deciduous shrubs and forgetting about until it emerges at a time when the garden lacks interest. Both purple and yellow forms are grown. The leaves appear after the flowers.

C. speciosus – the 10cm (4in) pale blue flowers with golden yellow anthers appear in mid-autumn; this is the true 'autumn crocus', but a pure white form and other sports exist.

C. tomasinianus – the flowers open into flat, almost dish shapes about 7-8cm (3in) above the ground in late winter. The leaves appear at the same time as the flowers. The purple varieties are most frequently grown.

C. vernus – the true wild species is seldom cultivated but it was from this form that all the large crocuses originated, and these at one time were the only forms which were readily available. The flowers consist of spoon-shaped petals, in a range of shades of yellow, blue and white and grow up to 12cm (5in) tall in late winter and early spring. The dark green leaves emerge with the flowers and are the same height or taller at the time that the plants are in bloom.

Crocuses
Planting time Corms should be planted immediately that they are obtainable in late summer/early autumn.
Aspect Any well-drained position. Prefers a sunny location, but can be planted under deciduous trees and shrubs, including bushes that have low-growing branches.
Space For naturalizing they should be placed no further than 7-10cm (3-4in) apart. As edging for borders they may be planted at twice this distance.
Planting depth 7-8cm (3in).
Height Depending upon species about 6-12cm (2½-5in).
Flowering period Depending on species, mid-autumn to early spring.
Uses Planted singly or in small, close-packed groups in alpine gardens, for naturalizing under deciduous trees and shrubs in grassed areas, and used as an edging to formal display beds. Also for forcing in bowls.
Propagation Cormlets.
Pests and Diseases Generally they are trouble-free but may be attacked by gladiolus dry rot.

Tulips

Tulips originate from Turkey and Asia and have been prized in Europe for over 300 years, with single bulbs changing hands for vast sums of money. They prefer an open aspect and should not be planted under trees, as only the earlies will have finished growing by the time that the deciduous trees are getting the new season's leaves.

Tulips make ideal bedding displays and are used extensively for this purpose. Use only one type for each display, which will ensure that all the blooms are in flower at the same time.

Tulips require a slightly alkaline soil, so acid ground should be given a very light dusting with lime prior to planting. Originating from a warmer climate, it is necessary to modify the general method used for growing native bulbs and those from the cooler countries. Unlike the majority of spring bulbs, tulips benefit from being lifted each year and are definitely not a subject for naturalizing. They should be dug up when the foliage has turned yellow and died back. Allow the bulbs to dry in the sun before storing in a cool dry place. Replanting should be delayed until mid- to late autumn to avoid the bulb prematurely starting into growth. Early shooting is not to be encouraged as growths that are too well advanced may be cut back by severe frosts.

Like many other bulbs there are numerous varieties, which have been categorized into fifteen divisions, the most popular of which are listed below.

The wide range of colours and flowering forms makes the tulip ideal for planting with a range of plants to flower in mid-spring. Here they are seen with that old favourite, the forget-me-not.

Spring-flowering bulbs should be stored during the summer in trays stacked in such a way that the air can circulate. Inspect regularly to ensure that there is no deterioration in the stock.

Popular Varieties

Single earlies – as the name implies these are the first to bloom, appearing in gardens from early spring onwards. They are extensively grown under glass to produce early flowers. Height varies from 20–40cm (8–16in) and the blooms have a tight goblet shape measuring 7–10cm (3–4in) across.

Double earlies – these grow to 30–37cm (12–15in) and should not be confused with the late doubles, which are far larger, possessing a denser head and petals and flowers that are far rounder than the early version. Double earlies are available in yellows, whites, deep red, purples and pinks as well as multicolours.

Rembrandt

Darwin

Parrot

Retroflexa

There are many different types and colours of tulip, each possessing its own special charm.

Tulips
Planting time   Mid- to late autumn.
Aspect   Sunny position – not in shade or under trees.
Space   15-25cm (6-10in).
Planting depth   15cm (6in).
Height   45-75cm (18-30in) depending upon variety. Kaufmanniana hybrids only grow to 15-20cm (6-8in).
Flowering period   From mid-spring to early summer.
Uses   For bedding, cut flowers, and in containers. Also for forcing.
Propagation   Bulblets.

Darwin tulips – are the best-known tulips, appearing in innumerable park displays. The flowers which appear in late spring have a goblet shape. They grow to about 60cm (2ft tall), with blooms that are 10cm (4in) across when open.

Mendel tulips – these are singles produced by crossing single earlies with Darwins, and these three divisions are probably the closest amongst the tulips with their separation causing the greatest confusion. The blooms of the Mendels, which appear in mid-spring, have a somewhat more rounded appearance than the others. The flowers are up to 12cm (5in) across and are carried on stems 45cm (18in) tall. They are available in all the colours of their parents.

Triumph – another mid-season bloomer, characterized by the almost angular look to the blooms compared with the gentle curves of many of the other varieties. As with the Mendels they are the result of crossing single earlies with lates. Colours include red, orange, gold, purple and pink. The 10cm (4in) across flowers are carried on 45cm (18in) stems.

Darwin hybrids – these have resulted from crossing Darwin tulips with a wild species. The result is what many people consider to be some of the most spectacular of all tulips with exceptionally bright colours, deepest shades of gold, yellow, purple and rose being amongst the most popular. The 15cm (6in) flowers are carried on 60cm (2ft) stems. The colours include pink, red, purple, yellow and bicolours.

Lily-flowered tulips – these have pointed petals that grow inwards from the base in a gentle curve before reflexing outwards, giving the blooms a waist, with the centre of the column narrower than both the base and the top. The stems grow to an average 50cm (20in) with the blooms 15cm (6in) at the opening. The best colours are the pinks, reds, yellows and whites. Blooms mid-season.

Cottage tulips – amongst the oldest forms in cultivation, these are characterized by the arrowhead-shaped petals, which in many varieties have a green back. Available in all the usual tulip colours. A large plant growing up to 90cm (3ft), with flowers 10cm (4in) across. Flowers from mid-spring onwards.

Rembrandt tulips – these are the varieties so often seen in the old Dutch Masters' still life paintings. They are basically Darwin tulips with the much-prized broken colours consisting of flashes of a dark shade on a far lighter background. Other details are similar to those of Darwin tulips.

There are even low-growing tulips, such as Tulipa praestans, which are ideally suited to growing in rock gardens. T. praestans *is not recommended, however, for bedding displays where it tends to be outshone by the taller growing forms.*

Tulipa kaufmanniana, *a dwarf variety which is ideal for including in tubs, containers or hanging baskets.*

Parrot tulips – these are the monsters of the group with blooms which may be up to 20cm (8in) across carried on 60cm (2ft) tall stems. The blooms appear in mid- to late spring and can be purple, orange, yellow, white or blue-purple. The variety 'Fantasy', in the most delicate shade of pink, is one of the most popular of all tulips. The very open twisted petals, which bear no resemblance to the globular shape of the Darwins, have irregular crimped edges.

Double lates – these also have very large flowers 20cm (8in) carried on 60cm (2ft) stems. The many-petalled blooms appear similar to those of peonies. Available in virtually all the tulip colours. They do not bloom until late spring.

Kaufmanniana tulips – these are the most delicate members of the tulip family, the nearest that there is to true miniatures; they only grow to 15-20cm (6-8in) with finely pointed petals producing an open bloom measuring 7cm (3in) at the widest point. The pinks and reds are amongst the most popular in this group, which is extremely useful for growing in containers. Flowers in mid-spring.

Hyacinths

The most frequently grown form of the hyacinth consists of a single spike, which can contain over a hundred five-petalled, bell-shaped flowers. Two distinct types of hyacinth are commonly available, bulbs for forcing and those for growing in the garden. The two are not different varieties, rather the different descriptions refer to the manner in which the bulbs were prepared; most cultivars can, depending upon their previous treatment, be used for either purpose, but once purchased it is not advisable to interchange the roles.

Hyacinths, with their large flowers and exquisite perfume that can be detected far away, are one of the finest of all the spring-flowering bulbs.

frequently grown single-stemmed varieties are often referred to as Dutch hyacinths.

Roman hyacinths are derived from a different species and have two or three stems, each carrying flowers, which are more loosely packed on the stalks. They are not usually prepared for forcing. Hyacinths do not need to be lifted after flowering but the seed heads should be removed and leaves and bulbs protected with slug pellets.

Snowdrops

A British native, capable of withstanding the severest weather conditions, that spreads rapidly once it has become established.

Snowdrops
Planting time   As soon as the flowers have died in mid-spring.
Aspect   Partial shade.
Space   Place small clumps of about six plants in groups a foot apart.
Planting depth   Return the plants to the same depth that they were originally growing in the soil.
Height   15cm (6in).
Flowering period   Mid-winter to mid-spring.
Uses   Naturalizing in open sites and under deciduous trees, for planting individual bulbs for spots of colour in rock gardens.
Propagation   Allow bulbs to remain and divide naturally. When groups are too large, lift the clump, divide and transplant.
Pests and diseases   Usually not a problem.

Usually larger bulbs are selected for forcing and are prepared using special heat treatments. This effectively confuses their biological clocks so that when they are received they are primed to start the growth process several weeks before untreated bulbs. Specimens for growing in the garden are stored naturally at atmospheric temperature. The colour of the outer skin of a hyacinth bulb will give you some indication of the shade of the flower. White and yellow flowering bulbs have a dried outer skin which is white in colour, whilst those of red and blue shades tend to possess a metallic, reddish-blue sheen.

Flowering times differ depending upon the various cultivars, and this is most noticeable with bulbs for forcing. The most

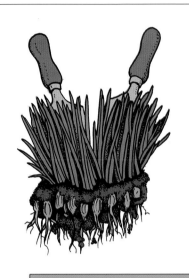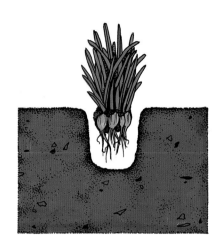

Transplanting in the green Snowdrops can be purchased as small growing clumps from florists or specialist suppliers. Plants intended for transplanting as a method of propagation or because they have become overcrowded can be treated in the same way. Divide the clumps into groups of about six bulbs, retaining the foliage undamaged. Plant to the same depth as that at which they were previously growing. Firm the soil around the plants with your fingers to ensure that there are no air pockets that could trap water.

Snowdrops have an outer ring of three petals and an inner circle of three smaller petals. The inner petals have green markings at the edge nearest to the opening of the flower. Snowdrops are very thin-skinned bulbs that prefer not to be disturbed, although they can be transplanted quite happily if they are planted 'in the green' just after they have flowered. They can be transplanted and divided at the same time, but should never be dug up after the greenery has died back. Consequently they should be planted where they can remain undisturbed for years in a site where they will increase annually to form large clumps. They are ideal for growing in orchards, on banks and under hedges. Snowdrops should not be planted in locations that receive full sunlight because in their resting period during the summer they may be baked dry if the soil becomes very hot even though they are underground. Do not remove the seed heads from naturalized snowdrops; being native wild species they will breed true to form from seeds, which will increase the number of plants in a pleasant random manner. Only two forms are in general cultivation.

The common snowdrop *Galanthus nivalis* – the species normally on sale as bulbs. *Galanthus nivalis* 'Flora plena' – a sport of the above form usually only available from specialist suppliers and sold 'in the green'. It is commonly referred to as the double snowdrop.

Leucojums
Planting time   Bulbs should be planted in early autumn or transplanted in late spring after the leaves have died back.
Aspect   Semi-shade. They grow well against west-facing walls, where they do not get the sun until later in the day.
Space   In small groups of about three or four bulbs about 30cm (1ft) apart.
Planting depth   7cm (3in).
Height   30-45cm (1-1½ft).
Flowering period   Mid- to late spring.
Uses   In permanent mixed beds.
Propagation   Leave bulbs in the ground to divide and self-propagate.
Pests and diseases   Usually not a problem.

Leucojum or Snowflake

Often confused with snowdrops, to which they are distantly related, the most obvious difference is the size of the bell-shaped flowers, which may be 2-3cm (1in) in length. With snowflakes, all six petals are of the same size, whereas they differ in snowdrops. Snowflakes are larger plants, and bloom later in the season; one of the three species cultivated even blooms in July. Leucojums may be planted as bulbs, or you can wait until the leaves have died back and transplant to the new situation. The plants should be left for several seasons until the production of flowers decreases; then lift, divide and transplant after flowering is completed.

Alliums – The Ornamental Garlics

The onion family's most distinctive characteristic is the spherical or flat blooms made up of several individual flowers. The leaves are either hollow round tubes (onions) or flat oval shapes (garlic). When cut or damaged they emit the familiar pungent odour typical of the family, making them totally unsuitable for cut flowers. They bloom mainly in early summer and so are intermediate between the spring and summer bulbs. It is usual to grow alliums as part of a mixed bed, siting them in a sunny location. They will form large clumps that should be divided regularly; this can be conveniently performed as soon as the first green shoots emerge during the spring. Alliums do well on all types of soil, including chalk, providing that the ground is well drained. It is the true wild species rather than artificially created garden hybrids that

Alliums
Planting time   Early to mid-autumn.
Aspect   Sunny, fully exposed location. Not suitable for growing in shaded areas.
Space, planting depth, and height   Varies depending upon species: consult cultural instructions usually supplied with the bulbs.
Flowering period   Mainly early summer, with a few species flowering in mid- to late spring.
Uses   Planting in mixed beds.
Propagation   Bulbils or seeds.
Pests and diseases   White rot.

are usually grown. They do not lend them-selves to formal layouts.

Popular Varieties

A. caeruleum – this species grows to 60cm (24in) high and produces deep blue flowers during early and mid-summer.

A. giganteum – the monster of the group, with the flowering spike growing to 120cm (4ft), carrying an 8-12cm (3-5in) magenta flowering sphere that appears in late spring/early summer.

A. moly – this grows to only 30cm (12in), so is suitable for the front of a bed or in a rock garden. The yellow flowers, which are dish-shaped, appear in late mid-summer.

A. neapolitanum – this is one of the earliest of all the *Alliums* and flowers in mid-spring. Unfortunately it is one of the least spectacu-lar, with white star-like flowers arranged in a dish shape 3-4cm (1-1½in) across. The flowering spike grows to 30cm (12in), which is only just above the clump of light-green, strap-like leaves. It blooms from mid- to late spring.

A. ostrowskianum – this plant grows to 30cm (1ft) tall with very loose, spherical, delicate rose-pink flowers 2-4cm (1-1½in) across. It flowers during early summer.

A. siculum – another very popular species with bell-shaped flowers up to 10cm (4in) across carried on 1m (3ft) spikes.

Fritillaries

A group of bulbous plants characterized by their drooping, bell-shaped flowers. The bulbs consist of fleshy scales and have a hollow centre. They will grow in any soil (including chalk), providing that it is well drained and rich in humus. Great care should be taken not to damage the delicate tissue of the bulbs, which do not like being out of the soil for prolonged periods. The bulbs should always be planted on their

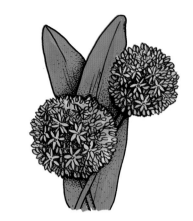

The alliums. The ornamental onions have either tight spherical inflorescences or open blooms, in either case made up of a collection of several small star-shaped flowers.

side so that the aperture does not trap and retain water, which would cause the bulb to rot. Only two species are commonly grown out of doors and both will flower in mid-spring.

Fritillaria imperialis (crown imperials) – these consist of a tall 60-75cm (2-2½ft) spike with leaves growing from the stem itself for half its length. This is surmounted by the crown, consisting of six to ten bell-shaped flowers beneath a tuft of leaves. It is available in red, orange and yellow.

F. meleagris (snake's-head fritillary) – British native, its preferred location is in damp meadows. It grows to a height of 22-37cm (9-15in). Cultivars of the species exist; the main colour, closely related to the naturally occurring form, is purple-spotted dark (almost black) chequering. White hybrids, with or without green veins, are also popular.

Anemones

Spring-flowering anemones are tuberous-rooted, unlike the summer varieties which are fibrous-rooted perennials. Anemones are characterized by their open, dish-shaped flowers. The tuberous forms prosper in open locations on any well-drained soil, including those high in chalk. Two types of tuberous-rooted, spring-flowering anemones are commonly grown. The flowers of each are borne on 22-30cm (9-12in) stems in the early spring.

De Caen anemones – these are singles obtainable in red, deep blue and (less commonly) white. Prized as cut flowers, the plants may produce several stems over a fairly long period if cut regularly.

St Brigid anemones are really the double version of the De Caens with an additional ring of inner petals. The more spectacular flowers have to be paid for by a drastic

Anemones
Planting time For spring flowering, plant in early to mid-autumn. Far less restricted in their season than other tuberous-rooted plants, they can also be planted during the spring to produce a succession of blooms.
Aspect Open, sunny position.
Space Plant 15cm (6in) apart.
Planting depth 3-5cm (1-2in).
Height 15-30cm (6-12in).
Flowering period Mid-spring, or with successive planting, throughout most of the year.
Uses In mixed borders, but not suited to formal displays.
Propagation Division.
Pests and diseases The main danger is from slugs and snails, and plants should be protected by pellets as soon as the shoots emerge.

reduction in the number of blooms. Available in the same colours as above.

Muscari (Grape Hyacinths)

These consist of several minute, mid-blue, bell-shaped flowers carried on a stalk 7-10cm (3-4in) tall. They appear to be a miniature version of the hyacinth to which they are related but do not possess the wide

The familiar bell-shaped flowers are carried on stalks high above the clumps of strap-like leaves. This is a flower to be appreciated grown in mass amongst trees in semi-shaded, slightly damp locations. The blue haze of a bluebell wood is one of the true delights of spring, but they do not have sufficient presence to be grown as individual flowers. Bluebells have true bulbs that do not possess an outer skin of dead leaf scales to protect them, which means that they are only able to survive out of the ground for very short periods of time, a matter of days at the most. Once they have been dug up they will either dry out rapidly

Muscari (Grape Hyacinths)
Planting time   Early to mid-autumn.
Aspect   Open, sunny position.
Space   Group close together – individual bulbs should be set 5cm (2in) apart.
Planting depth   5-7cm (2-3in).
Height   7-10cm (3-4in).
Flowering time   Mid- to late spring.
Uses   In mixed beds and for picking and use in miniature floral arrangements.
Propagation – Self-sown seed or division.
Pests and diseases   Generally trouble-free, but may be attacked by slugs.

Bluebells
Planting time   Late spring.
Aspect   Prefers slight shade, such as under trees.
Space   Plant groups of six bulbs together with greenery about 15cm (6in) apart, or closer if there are more bulbs available.
Planting depth   7-10cm (3-4in).
Height   30cm (12in).
Flowering period   Mid- to late spring.
Uses   Naturalizing only.
Propagation   Seed or division.
Pests and diseases   Trouble-free.

range of colours; only blue and occasionally white forms are grown. The bulbs, which should not be disturbed for several years, are ideal for placing at the front of the border.

Bluebells

These should not be confused with the Scottish bluebell, which is a *Campanula* species (sometimes referred to as a harebell).

or develop fungal growth. The only way that bluebells can be transplanted is 'in the green' immediately after flowering. Once established, they spread rapidly and tend to become invasive, so they are not suitable for inclusion in mixed beds. Two naturally occurring sports are whitebells and pink-bells. All three colours may be purchased from specialist suppliers.

Scillas

Fast becoming popular, these low-growing, ground-hugging plants are fully hardy and once established produce a profusion of blue, star-shaped flowers in the early spring, making them ideal subjects for alpine gardens. Undemanding, they are equally at home in most soils and prosper in both full sunlight and partial shade.

Bulbs such as miniature daffodils, scilla and snowdrops can be planted in rockeries, but unlike normal rooted plants they require an area of rock-free soil in which to grow. Select such an area, dig out a hole and plant the bulb in the normal way.

Scillas
Planting time Early to mid-autumn.
Aspect Open or partially shaded.
Space Plant individual bulbs in groups any distance apart you choose. Within the group the bulbs should be set 5cm (2in) apart.
Planting depth 5cm (2in).
Height 10-15cm (4-6in).
Flowering period Early to mid-spring.
Uses In rockeries or at the front of beds.
Propagation It is not usual to disturb scillas but they can be propagated by lifting the bulbs after they have flowered and replanting in the early·autumn.
Pests and diseases No special problems.

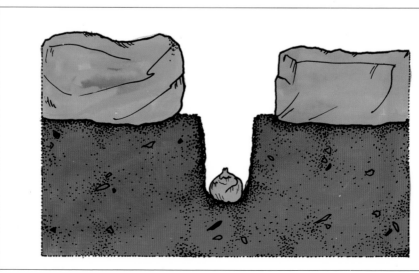

5 • SUMMER BULBS

We inevitably think of spring as the season of the bulb, but there are several bulbs and bulb-like structures that are indispensable to the summer garden. Whilst spring bulbs that flower during or just after the harshest time of the year can survive in the ground all the year round, enjoying their dormant season during the plant-friendly summer months, the summer-flowering species cannot.

Because a bulb flowers and prospers during the summer months it does not follow that it will survive the winter at rest underground where it will need to be able to withstand the combined effects of possible flooding and hard frosts.

There are two groups of summer bulbs, those which can be left in the ground undisturbed and the tender subjects. The latter originate from countries with warmer climates so they can survive and prosper out of doors during the summer but must be artificially overwintered if they are to remain alive and produce flowers in subsequent seasons.

Overwintering Summer Bulbs

Summer bulbs can generally be left in the ground until the first frosts, which will usually be mild. This will kill the vegetation but is unlikely to penetrate the soil and damage the swollen roots or stems below ground level.

Immediately that the greenery dies, cut the stems off at about 15cm (6in) above ground level. The roots should be lifted with a fork, taking care not to damage them. Transfer the bulbs together with the damp soil which does not come away easily from them, to a frost-free area – a conservatory, greenhouse or spare room. If the stem tissue above the root contains a large amount of sap the bulb must be hung upside down to ensure that the liquid drains out.

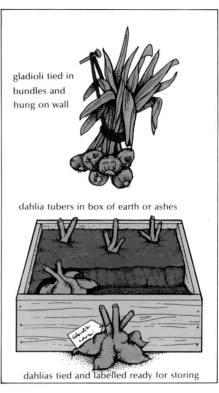

gladioli tied in bundles and hung on wall

dahlia tubers in box of earth or ashes

dahlias tied and labelled ready for storing

To overwinter tender, summer-flowering bulbs you must find a cool, dry, frost-free room to store them. Suspend or place in trays to avoid the still, humid air that causes rots.

When the current year's growth has died back it should be removed. With your hands clear away the by-now dried soil. Carefully examine each bulb for signs of damage or fungal infection; the latter is often seen on the surface of dormant tissue as brown or black spots with or without pitting. Damaged material should be removed by means of a clean cut. Any roots suffering severe fungal infection should be destroyed.

Store the bulbs in brown paper bags, carefully marking the name of the bulb on each bag. Never place the bulbs in polythene which will cause them to sweat, simultaneously dehydrating the bulb and creating the humid conditions that encourage fungal infection to set in. Stored bulbs should be inspected regularly throughout the winter period and any showing signs of disease must be discarded.

As with all bulbs, summer-flowering varieties will recommence growth below ground long before any activity is seen above. During early spring the bulbs, now no longer dormant, will start back into growth by producing pale yellow shoots. Depending upon species it is usually advisable to plant the bulbs in pots, allowing them to grow in a cool greenhouse until all danger of frost has passed and it is safe to plant them out of doors.

Instant effects can be produced by transferring hardened-off pot-grown plants directly into the turf from which a core of soil has been removed. The plug can be removed after flowering to avoid the problem of having to allow the leaves to die back in the lawn.

Hardening Off

Prior to setting out in the spring, any plants that have been raised or started out of doors must be hardened off – acclimatized to the harsher environment outside. This is necessary not only to reduce the stress the plant experiences as a result of transplanting, but also to reduce the rate of growth and toughen up the individual cells. About a fortnight prior to the time that it is intended to set the plants out, they should be stood out of doors in the morning. If there was a late frost delay the operation until such time that the temperature has risen well above freezing point. On days when there are strong cold winds, either find a suitable sheltered spot or keep the plant indoors, as the leaves are still extremely delicate and can very readily become scorched. Bring the plants back indoors during the evenings. If you possess a cold frame place the pots in it. During the day remove the lights, replacing them at night. After a fortnight the plants will be fully hardy and ready for planting out into their summer quarters.

Dahlias

Dahlias are tuberous-rooted, with the ability to produce flowers continually from mid-summer through until the first frosts, making them the ideal source for cut flowers, as well as being useful in landscaping terms, providing height and mass in the border. Four plants should provide sufficient blooms for cut flowers for the average household, but there are so many different forms and colours that you may choose to grow many more.

The dahlia root consists of a number of swollen, finger-like structures attached to the previous year's stem.

Tubers should be planted in the ground in the year they are purchased without any attempt to propagate or divide them. One-

Dahlias
Planting time Mid-spring for tubers; as soon as all danger of frost has passed for rooted cuttings.
Planting depth Tubers 10cm (4in), rooted cuttings 5cm (2in).
Height Pompoms grow to 60cm (2ft) while the tallest of the large decorative varieties can reach 1.5m (5ft).
Flowering period Mid-summer until the first frost.
Uses Can be grown in nursery beds for cut flowers or as part of a mixed bedding scheme.
Propagation By root division or cuttings.
Pests and diseases Earwigs and aphids.

of the main pests of dahlias are earwigs, which climb up the flower stems and chew the petals, often leaving them with a fringe-like appearance. Fill a flowerpot with dried grass, invert and place on the top of the spike. Inspect each morning for earwigs, which will hide during the daytime in the cover provided. Do not kill the earwigs, transfer them to another part of the garden as far away from the dahlias as possible, where the omnivores will consume several other garden pests.

Flower buds develop at the end of the stems, which emerge from the main growth; just below them a secondary pair of buds begins to form. If all three buds are allowed to remain it will result in the plant producing a large number of short-stemmed flowers totally unsuitable for cutting. Disbudding will reduce the number of

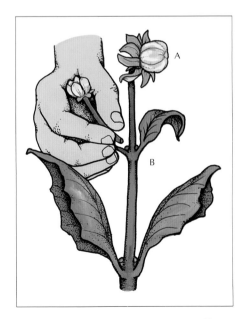

Dahlias flower from a main stem supported by two secondary buds. Either leave just the main bud (a), or pinch out the main bud and allow the two secondary buds to develop (b).

year-old and older roots can be used to provide extra stock in one of two ways – by cuttings or by root division. Use the latter if you do not have access to a greenhouse.

Dahlias are amongst the most prolific producers of foliage and flowers in a season and require a loam-rich soil to which a general fertilizer has been applied at the rate of 50g/sq m (2oz/sq yd).

Place a stake by the side of the plants and tie the plants to it to provide support. One potential flowers but will direct all of the plant's energies into producing large, long-stemmed blooms from the remaining buds. Disbudding can be done in two ways. For really monster blooms on tall, thick stalks remove both of the secondary buds; for twice the number of only slightly smaller flowers – the reduction in size is far less than you would think – pick out the main stem just above where the two secondaries are beginning to form; this will allow both of the back-up buds to develop into large, strong, cuttable blooms.

Dahlias will be cut down by the first frosts, the soft tissue becoming black in colour. The roots should be lifted and over-wintered as described above.

Dahlia Varieties

Single-flowered – this is the basic form but is seldom grown now. It consists of a central disc surrounded by a ring of overlapping florets.
Collarette – these are intermediate between the single form and the doubles, consisting of a central disc surrounded by a ring of small, insignificant, rudimentary petals with an outer ring of normal, well developed petals or florets.

All the other varieties described below are true doubles.

Anemone-flowered – these consist of a very dense centre of tubular petals, becoming increasingly open as they progress towards the outside, where the florets are flat and slightly reflexing.
Decorative – with these the petals are most densely packed at the centre, although this tends to be more in the shape of a cone with all traces of the central disc having dis-appeared. The distinguishing feature about this group of dahlias are the flat petals.
Ball – as the name implies, these are round with a slightly flattened top. Whereas with

The collarette dahlia has a very delicate inner ring of modified florets, which makes it one of the most delicate forms of this ever-popular flower.

other dahlias the blooms are set at 45 degrees to the stem, in the ball varieties they appear as a sphere resting on a spike.
Pompon – these are best considered as smaller versions of the ball dahlias. They are smaller plants and have far shorter stems than the other dahlias, making them more suitable for inclusion in mixed beds. The flowers are more suited to smaller floral decorations than bouquets.
Cactus – this is one of the most popular groups of all dahlias; the characteristic that sets them apart is that for most of their length the petals curve in on themselves to form a tube.
Semi-cactus – these are similar to cactus dahlias but the petals are in the shape of a tube for less than half their length.

In addition to the broad general groupings many of the types are further subdivided according to the size of the flower.

Gladiolus

Originating from corms, gladioli consist of a single flowering spike which has several six-petalled, individually trumpet-shaped flowers. The blooms open gradually from the bottom of the spike upwards over an extended period, making them the ideal flower for cutting mid- to late summer. Six to a dozen gladioli will provide incomparable cut flowers and no garden should be without what I like to call the 'Queen of the Bouquets'.

Gladioli need a rich soil with a sunny aspect. Turn the soil over in early spring, work some well-rotted manure or compost into the site and give a top dressing of compost. To achieve a succession of blooms for cutting, plant a batch of corms at fortnightly intervals from early to mid-spring. Stake the large-flowering hybrids and keep them well watered during dry spells. For bouquets cut the blooms when the first flowers at the bottom of the stems begin to open. The corms must be lifted and stored inside through the winter.

Gladiolus Varieties

Large-flowered hybrids – these grow to 60–100cm (2–3ft) with very thick, strong stems. The flowering part of the spike can be up to

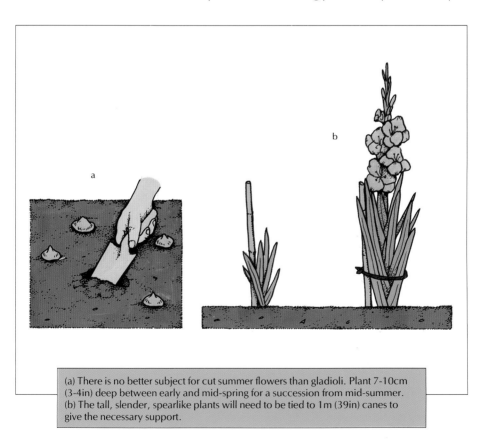

(a) There is no better subject for cut summer flowers than gladioli. Plant 7-10cm (3-4in) deep between early and mid-spring for a succession from mid-summer.
(b) The tall, slender, spearlike plants will need to be tied to 1m (39in) canes to give the necessary support.

60cm (2ft) long. The flowers are 10–20cm (4–8in) across and are tightly packed together. These are the monsters of the show bench and are the type to grow for cutting, but they do require staking, which can look out of place in the border.

Butterfly hybrids – these grow to a similar height as the large-flowered hybrids but with the closely packed individual flowers being 4–8cm (2–3in) across, at first appearance

Gladioli
Planting time   Early to mid-spring.
Planting depth   10–15cm (4–6in).
Height   Gladioli grow to 1m (3ft).
Flowering period   Mid-summer to early autumn.
Uses   In borders and for cut flowers.
Propagation   Cormlets.
Pests and diseases   Both thrips, which cause a mottling of the leaves, and aphids affect the growing plants and can even damage stored bulbs. Stored bulbs may also be infected with a number of rots and care must be taken to ensure ideal storage conditions.

they tend to be less striking. Yet any lack of size is compensated for by the delicacy of the blooms, which have strong complementary throat colours.

Primulinus hybrids – a smaller type only growing to 30–75cm (1–2½ft) and with flowers 5cm (2in) across. Unlike the other varieties there is a gap between the individual flowers, which gives the blooms an altogether subtler appearance. They are ideal for cutting, or discreetly supported they will give height to alpine and other low-lying landscapes.

Miniature hybrids – as the name implies these are the smallest members of the group, although the flowering stems reach a similar height to the butterfly types and the flowers at 3–4cm (1–1½in) across are only fractionally smaller. The individual blooms are close-packed.

Lilies

The name 'lily' is widely used to describe many flowers but should correctly be restricted to members of the *Lilium* genus. The bulbs of this group consist of several overlapping leaf scales tightly packed around the centre. Very many different hybrids have emerged in recent years. There is a classification system based mainly upon the species from which the hybrids were originally derived, and upon the features of the hybrids. The general characteristic of the *Lilium* species is that the flowers always have six petals, often with very prominent orange pollen-covered stamens. The flowers of the *Lilium* group vary from the trumpet-shaped forms such as *L. regale* through to those cultivars where the petals reflex back with the stamens protruding as the dominant feature of the pendulous blooms. Intermediate forms can display slight backwards curvature of the petals, whilst in others the petals open out fully to produce a flat bloom with the stamens once

One of the many lilies which provide colour, shape and, in some cases, exotic perfumes to the summer garden.

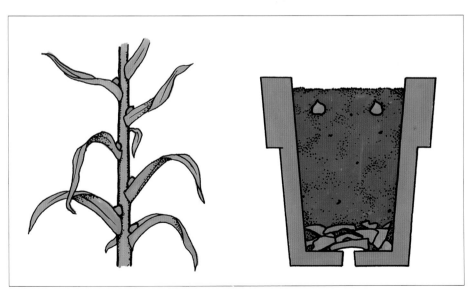

Some lilies form bulbils at the joints between stem and leaves. Remove the bulblets and pot in a peat-based compost. Continue to grow in the pot until they have become full-sized bulbs.

again prominent. Some forms, which can also be grown as pot plants for greenhouse or lounge, emit one of the most powerful and exotic of all plant perfumes.

Lilies prefer a rich, well-drained soil in an open position, where they will receive full sunlight, but will be sheltered from strong winds. Before planting the bulbs, work some well-rotted manure or compost into the ground. The bulbs can be allowed to remain in the soil throughout the winter. In cold areas, frost pockets or where draughts can be a problem, they should be given some protection in the early spring to protect the young, re-emerging shoots. Tall varieties should be discreetly staked with a bamboo cane.

Lilies are ideal subjects for growing in pots. Plant the bulb in a 20cm (8in) pot as soon as they are on sale in the shops in the spring. Use either a soil- or a peat-based compost. Place the pots out of doors in a cool but not cold position, which will ensure good root development rather than premature bud growth. When shoots appear and are about 10cm (2in) high, the pots can be brought into the greenhouse. Keep the compost well watered, giving a weekly feed with a liquid fertilizer at half the recommended dosage. Lilies will increase by the formation of additional bulbs around the main structure. These may be lifted and divided when the group becomes overcrowded. More rapid increase in the number of bulbs can be achieved by scale propagation.

Lilies
Planting time   Mid-spring.
Planting depth   Three times the depth of the bulb.
Height   1–1.3m (3–4ft).
Flowering period   Mid- to late summer.
Uses   For growing in groups in mixed borders.
Propagation   By group division, leaf scales or bulbils.
Pests and diseases   Emerging shoots should be protected from attacks by slugs. Lilies are vulnerable to a variety of pests and should if necessary be sprayed with a general insecticide recommended for the purpose.

Irises

There are several diverse forms in this very popular group of flowers. The large, familiar flag lilies all grow from rhizomes, which are swollen horizontal stems; they are also vegetative storage organs capable of generating buds, so in many respects are similar to tubers. Totally hardy, they do not require lifting in the autumn. The rhizomes tend to take up a half-buried position on the surface and will gradually lose their vigour; they should be propagated and stimulated by division every two years.

Varieties

There are two groups of bulbous irises.

Iris reticulata hybrids – these are spring-flowering bulbs and vary in height from 10–30cm (4–12in). They have the characteristic iris-shaped flowers, carried near to the

Spring-flowering irises
Planting time   Mid-autumn.
Planting depth   5cm (2in).
Height   10–30cm (4–12in).
Flowering period   Early spring.
Uses   Bedding containers, hanging baskets. Taller forms may be grown for cutting. Also suitable for forcing (*see* Chapter 6).
Propagation   By division.
Pests and diseases   Generally trouble-free.

Summer-flowering irises
Planting time   Early to mid-autumn.
Planting depth   10cm (4in).
Height   45–60cm (1–1½ft).
Flowering period   Early to mid-summer.
Uses   Mixed beds.
Propagation   By bulb division.
Pests and diseases   A variety of fungal attacks can occur. Treat by using a suitable proprietary fungicide according to the manufacturer's instructions.

Short spring irises and crocuses growing together in a tub. Planted containers can be raised in the cold greenhouse and set out in their final position when the flowers are in bud.

ground in early spring; they are also ideal subjects for including in containers.

Iris xiphium and others – the hybrids of these may be divided into three groups, sometimes referred to in their order of flowering as Dutch, Spanish and English irises. Although derived from different species they are very similar, varying in height from 30–60cm (1–2ft); they are available in blues, white and purples with pink and yellow hybrids also known. These are the summer-flowering bulbous irises.

Nerine

A most useful plant in any garden – almost indispensable in the autumn landscape – as the long-lasting, pink, reflexing, single open blooms first appear in late summer and remain until late autumn, surviving the first frosts. There is only one hardy species and all of the varieties developed so far tend to be similar. A true hardy perennial, once

Nerines
Planting time   Early to mid-spring.
Planting depth   10cm (4in).
Height   45cm (1½ft).
Flowering period   Late summer to late autumn.
Uses   General landscaping and floral decoration.
Propagation   The bulbs may be lifted and divided.
Pests and diseases   Generally trouble-free, but may suffer from thrips' infestation.

bulbous-shaped structures reminiscent of large tulips. The corms should be planted in late summer, when they will burst into almost instant bloom with a crocus-type flower. The leaves delay their appearance until after the flowers have died back and are often not seen until the spring. The flowers range in colour from white, through pale pink to red. Because all the materials necessary to create the bloom are contained within the corm itself the bulbs are sometimes grown as a novelty feature by standing aon a shelf without the provision of either soil or water. Bulbs treated in this way must be discarded after flowering.

The true autumn crocuses are really the earliest flowering species of the familiar spring crocus.

planted there is no need to lift the bulbs. With time they tend to work their way to the surface and should be protected by a mulch of compost given before the onset of winter. The usually visible bulb cluster will increase in size each year and should be left undisturbed until too many bulbs competing for too few nutrients results in a reduction in the number of flowers. Divide and replant the bulbs in the spring. They prefer an open position but can survive in a sheltered site, such as against a wall, which only receives the sunshine late in the day.

Colchicum

Colchicums are very similar in appearance to crocuses and are falsely termed 'autumn crocuses'. The difference between these two often-confused groups lies in the shape of the storage organ. True crocuses all have flat corms, whereas colchicums have

Brightly coloured begonias are popular not only as pot plants but as bedding plants outdoors.

6 • GROWING BULBS INDOORS

There are two distinct groups of bulbs which are grown indoors, hardy kinds identical to those that grow outside, and special tender species which need protection to survive.

Growing Hardy Bulbs

With hardy bulbs the main aim is to bring them into flower early, from mid-winter onwards, in order to advance the season and thereafter by means of successive plantings to provide colour in the household throughout the springtime.

Some bulbs, most particularly hyacinths, are sold specially prepared for forcing. Such bulbs are usually larger and more expensive, but for the extra money you will be getting specially selected bulbs, which have been heat treated to advance their growth cycle.

Clean-to-handle bulb fibre, usually peat or coir-based, is sold as a growing medium, but it has no advantage over a home-made, soil-based compost consisting of equal parts of loam and grit or sharp sand.

Once the bowls have been planted, and with the necks just exposed (as in the case of daffodils and hyacinths) or completely covered (for corms such as crocuses), the containers must be placed in a cool, dark

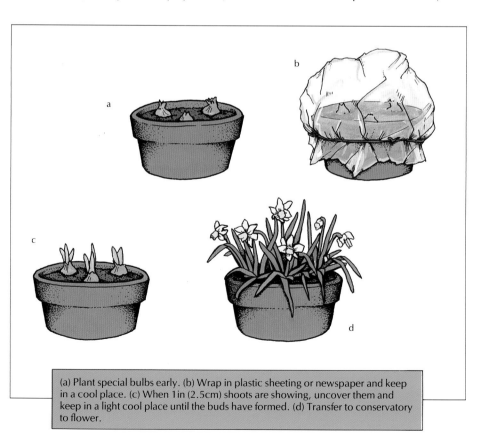

(a) Plant special bulbs early. (b) Wrap in plastic sheeting or newspaper and keep in a cool place. (c) When 1in (2.5cm) shoots are showing, uncover them and keep in a light cool place until the buds have formed. (d) Transfer to conservatory to flower.

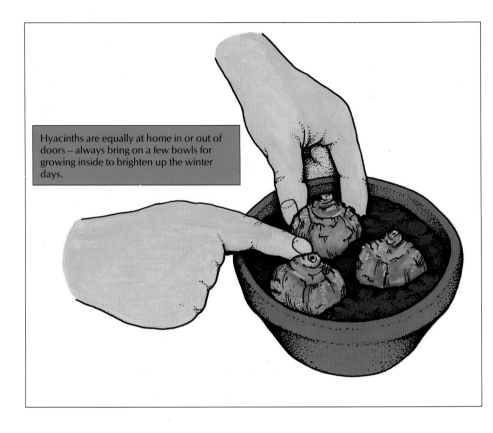

Hyacinths are equally at home in or out of doors – always bring on a few bowls for growing inside to brighten up the winter days.

place to allow the roots to develop, which in turn will trigger the shoots into growth. Choose a room in the house that is not affected by the central heating, outside in the garage, or if this is impractical, the containers may be buried with their tops level with the soil. Cover with a piece of black polythene to stop water from entering. Leave the bulbs undisturbed until the end of autumn by which time, depending upon species and variety, the first pale yellow pointed shoots will be beginning to appear. The pots should then be brought into a cool room where the temperature is not above 10°C (50°F) and allowed to remain uncovered for a further three weeks. After this period the bulbs may be brought into a temperature of 16°C (60°F). It is not advisable to keep the bulbs in a room at a higher temperature. As the temperature rises the whole growing process is speeded up, with the result that the flowers open far more quickly but also die much earlier. Bulbs grown in soil-based composts can be saved and grown on out of doors in future years, but it is seldom worth it as the combined effects of the heat treatment, the interference with their biological clocks, and the artificial indoor environment serve to weaken the plants to such an extent that they can take two to three years to recover.

Forcing is a technique designed to bring bulbs into flower earlier than is natural, yet bulbs also make excellent pot plants when they are raised to flower in the normal season. In the autumn simply plant unprepared· bulbs – they may be part of the propagated stock you raised yourself – in bowls and place under the staging of the greenhouse or in a shed. Alternatively they may simply be stood out of doors, provided that some protection is given to ensure that winter rains do not saturate them. Keep the compost moist. When the shoots emerge the bowls should be stood in a cool yet light area, and as the blooms start to open they may be brought into the house.

Growing Bulbs in Water

This is a novel method of cultivation, relying on the fact that all you are seeking to do is develop the buds and leaves already contained within the structure. The method is only suitable for true bulbs and is most successful with hyacinths, but it can be used with many types of narcissi, especially the early variety 'Paper White'. Suitably designed bulb glasses are available, consisting of a vase-shaped reservoir topped with a flat, dish-shaped portion that holds the bulb. If these are not readily obtainable, you can cultivate the bulbs in a wine glass, provided that it is fairly large and of a size to allow the bulb to rest on the rim. Place two or three pieces of charcoal at the bottom of the container to keep the water sweet before filling the vessel to the neck. Provide just enough water so that the base plate of the bulb alone is actually resting in the liquid. Do not allow any of the bulb above this level to become submerged or rotting will set in.

The bulbs and containers should be set aside in a cool and dark, but frost-free, position. Initially the containers should not need topping up with water as it is unlikely to evaporate very quickly under the conditions provided. As the roots develop they should remain in the water. If there is any danger of the roots drying out extra water

must be given. When the buds are 2-3cm (1in) in length they should be placed in the daylight, in a cool position such as on a windowsill. Once the bulbs have flowered they are unlikely to recover and so should be discarded.

Types of Hardy Bulb for Pot Culture

The main types of hardy bulb that are grown in pots include daffodils, narcissi, hyacinths, tulips and crocuses. Where specially prepared bulbs for forcing are available these should be bought so the first batch flowers around mid-winter, employing early planting techniques according to the general instructions provided in this chapter. Batches of unprepared bulbs can be placed in bowls at fortnightly intervals from early to late autumn to produce a succession of blooms during the spring.

Growing Tender Bulbs

Bulbs for forcing usually originate from colder climates and are frost hardy, whereas tender bulbs come from areas of the world that do not experience frosts. Consequently you will need to maintain the temperature for growing tender bulbs above freezing point permanently, and with some species it will be necessary to keep them significantly above this value. The method of cultivation also differs; bringing hardy bulbs into flower earlier depends upon creating an artificially early spring, whereas with tender subjects you are aiming to imitate their naturally warmer environment, allowing them to bloom in their natural season. Tender bulbs should not be started in the cold, neither should light be withheld from them, once they have begun to shoot.

Another important difference is that it is usual to save tender bulbs from one season until the next, when they will again be

Muscari and tulips blend together to form elegant displays in a variety of containers.

Once in bud they can be moved to the lounge, where the flowers can be enjoyed before being returned to their permanent home after blooming.

Frequency of repotting will depend upon species, but because of overcrowding and soil exhaustion in all cases it will be necessary to replant from time to time.

Pot Culture of Tender Bulbs

Ensure that the vessels have drainage holes. These holes should be covered with a piece of broken pot with the convex side uppermost. This will allow the excess water to escape while at the same time retaining all the compost in the container. Cover the bottom with a layer of soil-based compost of similar composition to that recommended for forcing. Place the bulb on the compost, put extra compost around the bulb and gently but firmly press it into position. Leave just the neck of the bulb protruding. Give small amounts of water at first, gradually increasing the quantity as the bulb bursts into growth. Pot-grown plants can only obtain their nutrients from the compost which rapidly becomes exhausted, and unlike with hardy bulbs, the aim is to build up continually and propagate bulbs for future years. Therefore it is important that they are continually fed with a weak liquid fertilizer, from the time that the shoots emerge from the neck until the time that active growth ceases.

Repotting Tender Bulbs

Allow the soil to dry out. Invert the open, wider end of the pot in the palm of your hand, then give the base a sharp tap. The whole of the contents of the container should come away easily into your hand. Place all of the contents on a newspaper and remove the bulb carefully from the dried, spent compost. Clean away any soil that remains around the bulb with your

raised inside in containers. This demands that special care is taken to achieve not only the relatively easy conditions necessary to induce flower formation in the first season, but an environment conducive to the development of bulbs for future years.

Since the bulbs will have to stay several months, possibly many years in a container it is necessary to create the right conditions. Ceramic or terracotta containers are more durable and worth the extra effort to seek out, compared with the shorter-lived plastic containers.

Do not neglect the plant after it has ceased flowering. As with hardy bulbs grown out of doors, this can be a critical time in the development of the following year's flowers. It is very important that you remove any developing seed heads and continue to water and feed after the flower has died. But as soon as the leaves begin to turn yellow, withhold the water and allow them to die back and ripen naturally.

Conservatories and greenhouses where the plants will enjoy a steady temperature coupled with maximum daylight are the ideal growing location for tender bulbs.

fingers. Repot as described for the initial planting in containers.

Popular Indoor Bulbs

Amaryllis (Hippeastrum)

The most popular of all tender bulbs, often sold as a complete kit consisting of bulb, bowl and compost. With no more effort than planting according to the instructions provided and the provision of water, the bulb will produce a 60cm (2ft) stem with up to four trumpet-shaped flowers 15cm (6in) across, with often a second spike, which is only slightly smaller, to follow. No instructions are usually provided on how to save the bulb, which can be coaxed into producing flowers annually, although they are usually smaller than those initially obtained from the prepared bulb.

Where it is intended to retain the bulb for growing on in future years it should be planted in soil-based compost in a 15-20cm (6-8in) pot, kept in a warm position about 15°C (60°F) and started back into growth by providing a little water. As the stem, with its arrowhead-shaped bud, and the leaves begin to emerge, start providing a liquid feed. This should continue until the leaves have died back after flowering is over. Withhold water to allow the bulbs to rest until the autumn, at which time they may be brought back into growth.

Amaryllises can be propagated from seed, although the hybrid varieties will not breed true. Allow the seed head to develop and ripen. Immediately the pods have acquired the colour of brown paper, gather and sow the large, flat seeds. Until the seedlings have actually produced a flower, which may take four to five years depending upon the conditions in which they are grown, they do not require a rest period. They should be maintained in growth all the

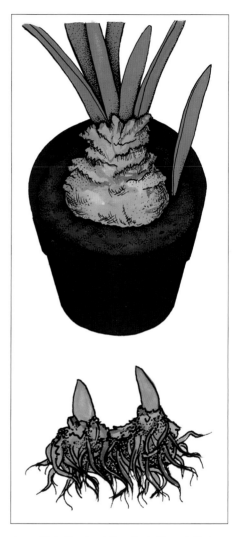

Amaryllis bulbs should be planted in pots that are only slightly larger than the bulb itself. The presence of an extra shoot indicates that a daughter bulb is forming.

year round by watering and giving a weekly feed with a liquid fertilizer at half the recommended strength. The flowers may be white, pale pink through to deepest carmine, or bicoloured, usually white shot with pinks or red. Double forms are now available.

Freesias

Freesias are as much prized for their perfume as for the beauty of the several trumpet-shaped flowers that emerge from the long, bending stem. Pot the bulbs in late summer in a well-drained, loam-based compost. Place four canes in a square formation at the edge of the pot. Evenly place string ties at three levels around the canes. This structure will retain the long, flowering stems which are incapable of supporting themselves. Maintain at a temperature of 5-10°C (37-45°F). Water and provide a liquid feed during growth. After the bulbs have flowered allow to die back naturally and withhold water. Once the growth has died back the elongated bulbs should be removed from the soil and allowed to dry out, when they will develop a dead, fibrous, protective layer around the outside. Any bulblets may be removed before repotting during late summer. Named varieties must be propagated from corms, but a range of colours can be obtained from seeds, which unlike many bulbous plants will yield flowers after just six months.

Gloxinia

These tuberous-rooted plants have several large trumpets of a velvet-like texture, which are 5-7cm (2-3in) at the opening. They are much prized as pot plants during the late summer months, when they produce a profusion of flowers. Good quality blooms may be obtained from seed sown in a peat-based compost in mid-to late winter and maintained at a temperature of 10°C (65°F) until germination is complete, and thereafter at 15°C (60°F). The seedlings sown in pans should be pricked out

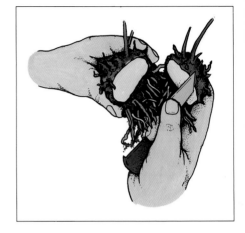

Tubers may be propagated by simply cutting them in half, ensuring that there are at least two buds in each piece.

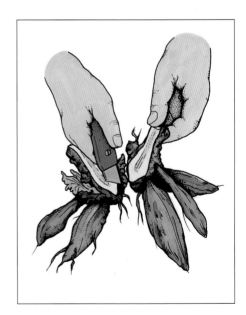

individually into 15cm (6in) pots as soon as they are large enough to handle. To produce blooms of named varieties which do not come true from seed, the previous year's tubers – or recently purchased stock – should be restarted into growth in late winter at 15°C. The tuber should be placed in the compost with the top flat surface exposed. Grow in a light position but shade from direct sunlight. The compost should be kept damp at all times but you must avoid overwatering. As soon as the first flower buds appear, give a weekly feed with a liquid fertilizer.

Once the plants have finished blooming in late summer, water should be withheld, the tubers dried off and stored for restarting into growth late next winter.

Begonias

Begonias form a very large group of plants, which from a gardener's standpoint may be divided into the following groups: tuberous-rooted, fibrous-rooted and the foliage begonias, whose flowers are insignificant (these are also fibrous rooted). Here we are only concerned with the tuberous-rooted forms, which have the most spectacular flowers. There are two main types of tuberous-rooted begonia, the standard upright varieties and the pendulous types, which are used in hanging baskets. The cultural methods are the same for both. Tuberous-rooted begonias must be started in heat, but from late spring onwards you have a choice: they can be retained in the greenhouse throughout their life or they can be planted out of doors.

The begonias should be started into growth in early spring by planting in a seed-box filled with a mixture of one part peat, one part grit and one part loamy soil at 15-18°C (59-65°F). When the shoots are about 2cm (1in) in height the tubers should be planted individually in 15-20cm (6-8in) pots and filled with the same compost as described above. For large, strong, upright plants, including the monsters shown in exhibitions, it is necessary to develop a large tuber to provide an abundant food

Begonias
Planting time   Early spring.
Planting depth   Plant the tuber flat on the surface with just the uppermost concave surface exposed.
Height   45cm (18in).
Flowering period   Mid-summer to mid-autumn.
Propagation   From the division of tubers when they become large enough or by shoot cuttings.
Repotting   Every year prior to starting the tubers back into growth.

supply but to allow only one, or at the most two, main stems to develop. Additional shoots may be removed and used for propagation.

The begonias are grown on either in the greenhouse or outside in the beds. Remove any seed heads as soon as they are seen in order to encourage the continual formation of flowers. During the autumn the leaves will begin to turn yellow; gradually reduce the water and allow the plants to die back. Prior to transplanting out of doors, plants should be hardened off in late spring by placing them outside during the daytime and bringing them back inside the greenhouse overnight. This will gradually acclimatize the plants, making it less stressful for them when they are finally transplanted out of doors. Such plants will prosper outside but they must be brought back inside before the first frosts occur in the autumn. Keep them in the greenhouse, geadually withholding water until the plants finally die back. Begonia tubers must be stored throughout the winter in conditions well above freezing point. When thoroughly dry, which may not be until around mid-winter, the tubers should be separated from the compost; any dead material and dry soil should be removed and the corms placed in brown paper bags labelled with the name of the variety for replanting at the beginning of spring.

Cyclamen

This is one of the most popular of all houseplants, and over recent years many different types have been developed, including bicolours, frilled petals, scented and variegated-leaf forms. To keep cyclamens you require a cool temperature – around 7°C (45°F) – but always above freezing point in a room where the air still

Cyclamen
Planting time Early autumn – start last year's tubers back in growth. (Corms of tender cyclamen are not on sale.)
Planting depth Leave just the surface of the corm exposed above the level of the compost.
Height Up to 40cm (16in).
Miniatures 15cm (6in).
Flowering period From autumn through until the spring.
Propagation By seed only.
Repotting Every year or every two years, depending on size.

contains its natural moisture level. Central heating dries out the air and produces too high a temperature, causing the leaves to yellow. At the first sign of yellowing the plant must be placed in a cooler but frost-free area. Kitchens and bathrooms often provide the ideal conditions for cyclamen. It is often possible to keep cyclamens in a dry atmosphere by standing the pot over a saucer filled with gravel, which is constantly topped up with water. This will not only provide the necessary moisture level but the constantly evaporating water will reduce the temperature in the vicinity of the plant.

The millions of pot-grown cyclamen on sale annually will all have been grown from seed sown in the current or previous year. It is often suggested that the plants should be replaced each year, but the old corms can be started back into growth, producing as good, if not better displays. It is not uncommon for corms of over twelve years of age still to be flourishing. Once the plants have stopped blossoming (by late spring), water should be gradually withheld. When the foliage has died back, the plants, still in their flowerpots, should be taken out of doors and stood on their side throughout the summer but the bulbs should not be allowed to dry out. In the autumn the bulbs can be brought back into the greenhouse and given small amounts of water as the shoots slowly unfurl into the first leaves. As the plant grows the watering should be increased gradually. Whilst in flower the plants should be kept damp and never allowed to dry out completely.

Division of cyclamen tubers is not recommended, and they do not produce offsets or bulbils, so propagation is by seed. Seeds may be sown during late winter to produce smaller flowering plants the following autumn, when it will be necessary to maintain a temperature of 15°C (60°F) during the germination and seedling stage. Alternatively sow in the greenhouse during early

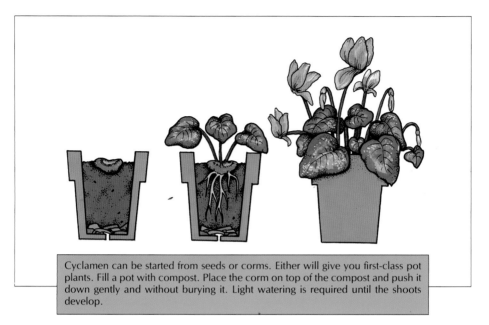

Cyclamen can be started from seeds or corms. Either will give you first-class pot plants. Fill a pot with compost. Place the corm on top of the compost and push it down gently and without burying it. Light watering is required until the shoots develop.

autumn when they will germinate at ambient temperature, but it will be necessary to maintain the value of 15°C throughout the winter. Such plants will produce larger corms for flowering a year after sowing.

Pleiones

These are true orchids, amongst the hardiest in cultivation and are no more difficult to grow than any of the other bulbous plants described. They have flowers consisting of five elongated petals, surrounding a trumpet-shaped centre with a fringed opening. They occur in the most delicate shades of pink, mauve, yellow and white – often bicolours – with the throats of the trumpets often spotted with darker shades. The pseudobulbs are best raised in the cool greenhouse and brought into the lounge when they are in bloom. They are epiphytic, growing naturally in the moss, leaf and other plant debris that collects at the forking of branches of a tree or on fallen mossy tree trunks.

In mid-spring prepare a compost of equal parts of peat, loam and grit or sharp sand and use it to fill a 15cm (6in) pot. Place five of the pseudobulbs in the pot. As subjects of the forest floor or growing in trees below the level of the canopy, they have not evolved to deal with direct sunlight and should be kept in a shaded, ventilated part of the greenhouse throughout the summer. Take care not to overwater in the early stages of the plants' development, but increase the moisture as the orchids increase in size. By mid-summer give a weak liquid fertilizer every ten days until early autumn. Water and feed should be withheld as soon as the leaves begin to turn yellow. They can be started into growth again the following spring.

In milder areas pleiones can be grown out of doors, but they should either be dug up and overwintered indoors or given some protection outside during the colder months. Before planting pleiones outside, select a site that does not receive direct sunlight and work a large quantity of peat into the soil.

7 • PESTS AND DISEASES

There are many organisms in nature that see your carefully grown plants as food sources. Some will infect the plants, allowing them to survive but reducing their performance, while others will destroy them completely. Such organisms can be broken down into two groups: pests, which are members of the animal kingdom, and diseases, which are caused by fungi, bacteria or viruses. As with all problems, prevention is better than cure, and the modern gardener uses an integrated system, whereby he relies on good horticultural practice to reduce the chance of problems developing in the first place.

Prevention

Keeping your plants free of problems will be much easier if you follow the guidelines below.

1. Thoroughly inspect all bulbs before planting, ruthlessly rejecting any that are not firm to the touch, as bruised or damaged bulbs are open to attack by bacteria.
2. Clear away outside surplus layers of dead skin, as these may be hiding a variety of predators.
3. Make sure that bulbs are grown correctly in good, fertile soil or compost – healthy plants are less vulnerable to attack.
4. Inspect plants regularly – infections noticed in the early stages are more easily treated and the spread of disease can be stopped.
5. Control pests immediately they are spotted. This is especially important with aphids, which can increase tenfold within one week at the height of the breeding season.
6. Keep the garden clean and tidy. Discarded rubbish provides hiding places for many pests, particularly slugs and snails.
7. Remove weeds; these can provide the initial food source before the pests move on to feed on the more tender cultivated plants, many of which have lost their natural resistance.

In spite of good, hygenic gardening practices, pests and diseases will occasionally develop, and you will probably need to control them by the use of pesticides and fungicides.

Warning Signs

1. Pieces eaten out of leaves and buds are an indication of the presence of chewing insects.
2. If there are dense colonies of virtually immobile creatures and no signs of chewing, these are likely to be sap-sucking insects, such as aphids.
3. If the plant wilts despite having sufficient water it is probably under attack from root-eating pests.
4. Soft, slimy tissue at the base or neck of a bulb is a sign of fungal rot.
5. If the bulb is soft to the touch, there could be various causes, including maggot infestation or rot.

Controls

Insecticides are used to deal with small animal infestations and may be used on both insects and other small garden invertebrates. There are two main classes of insecticide – contact insecticides, where the pest is destroyed by being sprayed with the chemical or by eating tissue that has been sprayed with it, and systemic insecticides, which enter the plant and are taken up by and kill sap-sucking pests.

Fungicides are used to control fungal infections. Bacterial garden infections are rare and do not respond to treatment, and there is no known control for viruses.

Pesticides are usually applied either as a

mist spray or a powder. They have to undergo vigorous testing and must be licensed before they can be put on sale. All garden chemicals must be used as recommended by the manufacturer, and you must read the label carefully and comply with its instructions rigidly.

Natural Controls

These are creatures that feed on pests and should be encouraged into the garden.

LACEWING FLIES

These are long, green insects with four lacy green wings. The adult flies are attracted to the nectar of many flowers, and this is their main food supply. They tend to lay their eggs on the plants on which they feed and the carnivorous larvae will consume enormous quantities of aphids at all stages in their development.

HOVERFLIES

These are yellow- and black-banded flies that mimic wasps to confuse their enemies. They take their name from their ability to hover in the air for long periods, seeking out a food source. The adults feed on both nectar and pollen, and like the lacewings lay their eggs where the predatory young can feed on aphids.

LADYBIRDS

This is a familiar group of beetles with brightly coloured outer wing cases, which may be red or black with spots or white and black chequered. Both the adults and the grey with red spotted larvae feed on aphids. Introducing ladybirds is probably the most effective natural method of controlling an aphid problem.

CARABID BEETLES

This is a group of predators that live in the soil, hence the alternative name of ground beetles. They prosper in undisturbed ground. They are mainly black in colour, although some forms have almost metallic green or purple sheens. Carabid beetles feed on a variety of soil pests, including larvae and pupae; the larger varieties even consume slugs.

Pests

Aphids

Aphids comprise a large group of sap-sucking pests that drain important nutrients from a plant, thus weakening it. A secondary problem is that they are often responsible for the transmission of viral infections, which weaken and destroy plants. They should be destroyed by spraying with a pesticide based on malathion, rotonene or pirimicarb.

Weevils

These are small beetles with prolonged snouts. The signs of weevil attack are small holes in the leaves or small, often rectangular signs of chewing around the edges of leaves or even the flowers themselves. Control by spraying with contact insecticides.

Earwigs

These have long, brown segmented bodies with clear, well-developed pincers attached to the head. Earwigs consume the petals of dahlias and similar flowers. They are omnivores and also have a beneficial role preying on other harmful pests. Trap them by placing an inverted flowerpot filled with hay on the top of a stake. This acts as a hiding place for the earwigs during the daytime. Once trapped, they may be removed to another part of the garden far away from the plants that they like to damage.

Eelworms are so small that they cannot be seen with the naked eye but they will infect bulbs in large numbers, causing reduction in size and distortion of both the leaves and the flower. Infected bulbs should be burnt.

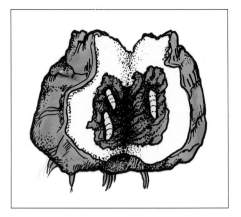

Eggs of narcissus fly laid in the neck of the bulb; these hatch and eat out the centre of the bulb.

Slugs and Snails

The gardener's number one enemy! These molluscs are active all year round and are especially mobile in wet weather, consuming any young and tender shoots they can find. Protect all emerging plants with slug pellets, as unprotected plants will soon be destroyed. You must be vigilant, as all the molluscs in the area do not feed every day, so there is always a new wave around the corner to attack your plants.

Narcissus Fly

This fly attacks hyacinths as well as daffodils. The female lays its eggs in the bulb after the leaves have died back, exposing the neck. The maggots eat away the inside of the bulb, which then becomes soft. Following an attack, the bulb will only produce thin leaves and no flowers. Avoid the problem by covering the necks of the bulbs with soil as soon as the leaves have turned yellow. If the problem persists, dust the soil around the bulbs with pirimophos-methyl.

Thrips

These cause yellow mottling of the leaves through secondary viral infections. A sign of the insects' presence are small, round, silver marks on the foliage. Treat with systemic insecticide or horticultural soft soap.

Infections

Viruses

There is a range of viruses that attack bulbous plants, particularly hyacinths and tulips; those that produce colour breaking of the petals cause no harm and such plants may safely be grown on. The appearance of yellow, white or brown markings on the leaves, however, is a sign of a viral infection that will impair the plant's performance, ultimately resulting in it failing to flower. Immediately that the problem is suspected remove and destroy the plants. If they are allowed to remain, sap-sucking pests will spread the disease to any other susceptible plants in the area.

Tulip Fire

So called because the edges of the leaves take on a brown appearance as though they have been scorched. Destroy the infected plant and spray other tulips in the vicinity with any general purpose fungicide.

Narcissus Fire

This fungal infection causes light brown spotting of the flowers and the leaves begin to show decay, followed by a grey mould. Pick any infected flowers to stop the spread of the disease and spray the leaves with a copper-based fungicide. If the problem persists, destroy the bulbs, plant new ones, and spray the leaves and buds when they emerge from the soil.

Gladiolus Dry Rot

This starts as small black marks on the corms, which quickly increase in size until they cover large areas. Where corms fail, they should be dug up and if they have black, pitted surfaces they must be destroyed.

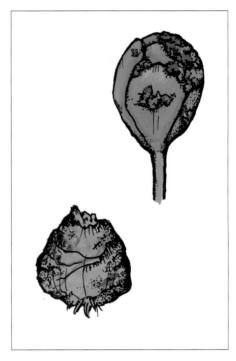

Tulip fire causes the leaves of tulips to appear as though they have been scorched; it is best to lift and destroy the bulbs.

White Rot

The bulb becomes soft and covered in a white, cotton wool-like fungus. Above ground the leaves become yellow and die. Destroy the infected bulbs, replacing with fresh bulbs planted in a different location the following autumn.

SUMMARY

Within the group described as bulbs are a whole range of plants. From the lowly growing species crocuses to the tall dahlias; from the fully hardy snowdrop that laughs at the worst of the winter to the tender gloxinia; from the pungent-smelling alliums to the sweet, seductively scented freesias: they all go to make up this group that we loosely refer to as bulbous plants.

There is not one month of the year when bulbs are not in flower and there are forms capable of withstanding most conditions, from the bitter cold of winter to the warm, dry conditions of the modern lounge. It is virtually impossible to garden without growing bulbs. Few homes are without pots of bulbs to lighten up the darkest days of the year. They are the most gardener-friendly of all plants and will almost always flower in the first season, even following the worst mishandling, but with a little care and attention they can be encouraged to give far better results. With a little help they will continue to flower for many years to come and can be successfully propagated to provide endless quantities of free bulbs for spreading around the garden or giving away to friends.

The culmination of the bulbgrower's effort: a beautiful spread of ground cover.

GLOSSARY

lb An underground storage organ. ere are various forms; the most common nsists of rudimentary leaf scales wrapped und a central bud.

lbil A small bulb-like structure, which underground and surrounds the main lb, as with the hyacinth, or above ground wing in the leaf axils of certain lilies.

rm An underground storage organ with ternal buds, which produce both the ots and roots. It differs from a bulb in it the latter is an underground bud, ereas a corm is an underground stem aring a terminal bud.

rmlet A small, immature corm that ms at the side of full corms. Cormlets are important method of propagating some ecies, particularly gladiolus.

iphytic Describes a plant that grows on other plant without being parasitic.

First generation crosses, whose prog-y are predictable and which have super-characteristics to either of the parents.

nus A distinct group of plants divided o a number of species.

rdy A plant capable of surviving out-ors all year round.

Hybrid A cross between any two species or varieties.

Naturalize To introduce a species to new conditions (such as your garden) and encourage it to grow there naturally.

Ovary The female cell of a plant.

Pollen The male cells of a plant.
Pseudobulb Literally 'false bulb'. The term is usually applied to bulb-shaped storage organs produced by orchids. They are not true bulbs because they do not consist of modified leaf scales surrounding a bud.

Rhizome A horizontally thick storage stem capable of generating leaves and roots. Certain types of iris possess rhizomes.

Scales The modified leaves that make up the bulbs of certain lilies.
Species A group of plants with common characteristics, distinctive from others of the same genus.
Sport A mutation from the normal type.

Tuber Underground stems of plants such as gloxinias or begonias, or swollen fleshy roots such as those of dahlias. Both groups need to be considered separately.

e daffodil remains one of the best-loved bulbs: this typical spring scene can easily be recreated .
a smaller scale in your own garden.

INDEX